DIRTY WORDS

A Study of Ephesians

By
Marc D. Royer Ph.D.

Dirty Words
A Study of Ephesians

Copyright © 2005

Marc D. Royer
All Rights Reserved.

Published by:
The Christian Resource Group
717 Bainbridge Place
Goshen, IN 46526
(574) 533-5133

ISBN 0-9705958-6-7
Library of Congress Control Number: 2005904252

Printed in the United States by Morris Publishing
3212 East Highway 30
Kearney, NE 68847
1-800-650-7888

OTHER BOOKS BY DR. MARC ROYER:

Secrets: Exposing, Resolving & Overcoming the Secrets We Carry with Us
Handling Death Dying and Grief
Rejection: Turning Your Lemons into Lemonade
Happiness in 30 Days or Less
Financial Freedom Starting Today
Practical Patience
The Development Manual Series
Volume I: A Study in the Old Testament
Volume II: A Study in the New Testament
A Study in the Life of David
A Study in the Prophets
Hell No!
Square Peg, Round Hole
Hocus Focus
The Spiritual Warfare Manual
Go Hard or Go Home
Removing the Obstacles to Effective Leadership Vol. 1
Instructions in Opposition Vol. 2
Soar! Effective Leadership Lessons Vol. 3

Write:
The Christian Resource Group
717 Bainbridge Place
Goshen, IN 46526

Or visit our web site at www.tcrg.org
Request These Titles from Your Local Bookstore

TABLE OF CONTENTS
(The 12 "Dirty Words" of Ephesians)

"Dirty Words"

A Study in the book of Ephesians

Dirty Words... Now that I have your attention, let's study Ephesians together! The "dirty words" idea represents twelve concepts found in Ephesians. They are concepts of the human journey that have become as shunned as actual foul language is to a child. It is not something we readily admit, but our lack of commitment to the twelve principles in Ephesians is obviously seen in our behavior. They become then, "dirty words" to us.

They don't have to be dirty words! The goal of our study of Ephesians is to develop some practical and applicable helps to make this human journey a success, as well as a successful spiritual journey. It is to this end we are committed.

"Dirty Words" (It even sounds dirty)!
****

Now that you are paying attention—let's look at these concepts.

Introduction: 1:1-14

"The Picture and the Photographer"

"Paul, an apostle of Christ Jesus by the will of God, to the saints in Ephesus, the faithful in Christ Jesus: Grace and peace to you from God our Father and the Lord Jesus Christ." Ephesians 1:1-2

This is a letter from Paul, whose tireless effort extends even from his prison cell, which would have imprisoned many in misery and self-pity. In his humanity, he would never know how deeply inspired his letter would be or that 1900 years later we would still be gleaning truth from it.

How often have you felt low or depressed?

How many times have you felt trapped?

How many times have you felt that you were not accomplishing anything?

You can be sure all these same feelings were experienced by the Apostle at this time, yet this letter from his heart, has turned the hearts of hundreds of thousands to Christ.

From his next few verses of chapter one (vs. 3-10), we see three tremendous truths of the human journey. We are even able to see the **why** for many of the things that do happen. We are given a divine illumination on the importance of the human journey to the spiritual world.

"The Picture"

EVERY MOVE COUNTS!

"Praise be to the God and Father of our Lord Jesus Christ, who has blessed us in the heavenly realms with every spiritual blessing in Christ." 1:3

If we would just pass over this verse by reading it quickly, we could miss its eternal truth. Any time the heavens or heavenly realms are mentioned in the Scripture, it would be wise for the Christian believer to stop and think awhile.

> **I want to know as much as possible about the place where I am going to spend eternity.**

Sadly, our modern idea of heaven is one of a celestial retirement center. The original languages give us a better picture of the heavenlies.

"Heavenly realms" gives us Paul's personal insight into the relationship between the human journey and its eternal destiny. Heavenly (epouramos) means "above the sky," that dimension that we cannot see but know is there. Realm (pantachos) is an expansive concept which means "universally everywhere." "Above the sky" and "everywhere" combined show us that heaven and earth are not separate in spirit—what happens in my life today affects the life above the sky. Every thought, word and action counts.

This concept that "every move counts for our eternal destiny" can supremely help us as we apply it on a moment by moment basis.

Before doing something, always ask yourself—"How does/will this affect me eternally?"

> # Every move counts.

OUR EVERY EFFORT IS FUTILE

"For He chose us in him before the creation of the world to be holy and blameless in his sight—In love he predestined us to be adopted as his sons through Jesus Christ in accordance with his pleasure and will—to the praise of his glorious grace, which he has freely given us in the One he loves." (1:4-6)

You are part of God's plan.

You were part of God's plan even before the conception of the world.

Not us--you. God knows you personally. We can't explain or understand it fully. Further, God existed before conception was possible. He invented it! None of His creation can figure how it is all possible.

In light of God's plan, **our human effort is futile.** We even have no control over our destiny—He predestined us. The term predestined comes from the word **(proorizo)** which means to "limit in advance." God has limited the eternal destiny to only those who have been "adopted as his sons through Jesus Christ." His adoption, according to the text, is enacted "in accordance with his will and pleasure." What is God's pleasure--"That no one will perish." What is His will? That we "confess with our tongue and believe in our heart, and we shall be saved."

Every effort done in our own strength is futile, but everything done as an adopted son of God is work done with eternal value. The adopted child of God should never do anything that does not have eternal value!

EVERY MINUTE OF LIFE NEEDS TO EXIST FOR CHRIST

"In him we have redemption through his blood, the forgiveness of sins, in accordance with the riches of God's grace—that he lavished on us with all wisdom and understanding. And he made known to us the mystery of his will according to his good pleasure, which he purposed in Christ to be put into effect when the times will have reached their fulfillment—to bring all things in heaven and on earth together under one head, even Christ." (1:7-10)

Much has been said and written about "blood." Some denominations have eliminated the "blood" songs from their hymnals. The blood is the sum total of the Christian existence, although maybe for a slightly different reason than is seen on the surface. The whole meaning of

9

"blood" is **haima,** or kindred. The bloodline showed the kinship of people. Through Christ we are the kinship of God again.

To illustrate his intensity, Paul uses the phrase "redemption through blood." Redemption (apolutrosis) means ransom paid in full. The Lord places a high value on humanity. Satan held us for ransom for Christ, and God paid it—in full.

Not only do we have this kinship through Christ, but also the forgiveness of sins. There are two types of sin addressed in the New Testament, the sin nature and unintentional slip-ups. The first type was the "ransom note" that was exchanged for Christ. It is the second type—unintentional (poraptoma)—that is mentioned here.

Do we still sin? It would be better asked, do we still have unintentional slip-ups? Yes we do! Are we held accountable for them? Not if we belong to Christ. The unintentional slip-ups no longer have life. Forgiveness (apsuchos) of sin means "lifeless." However, if we intentionally sin, we did not really take the kinship seriously.

Much of the picture is not yet complete or made known to us—that is all right. We know enough to keep busy! Every minute of your life matters--yield every minute of your life to Christ.

"The Photographer"

The first part of the introduction was "The Picture" as it showed the view of our human journey in light of our spiritual destiny. The photographer of this picture is the Holy Spirit. The Holy Spirit has taken an interesting development in Christian teachings today. From one end of the spectrum in evangelical Christianity we see the Holy Spirit rarely taught, to the other end of the spectrum where the Holy Spirit is sensationalized to the point of mysticism. The balanced believer must be in the center of the spectrum on the teachings of the Holy Spirit. The Holy Spirit is the activator of our Christian journey, and the actuator of our every spiritual experience. Without the Holy Spirit, there is no hope in applying these twelve concepts from Ephesians—without the Holy Spirit they will always be dirty words.

We are given three guidelines from Ephesians 1:11-14 for viewing the Holy Spirit as we study the concepts presented in this letter. These three guidelines can serve as a catalyst for growth. The intensity that follows in this entire study is a result of these guidelines, but it is for a purpose: conformity, preservation and insight.

CONFORMITY

"In him we were also chosen having been predestined according to the plan of him who works out everything in conformity with the purpose of his will...." (1:11)

Conformity is simple: God wants us to die out to everything except His will.

God will "limit in advance" his eternal kingdom to only those who die to everything except His will in their lives.

This spiritual experience is made by a definite decision or crisis point, followed by a process on which we work every day. But that is exactly God's will. The miracle is that God works out this journey individually with each of us.

11

This can only happen by His Holy Spirit. God's intentions for the Holy Spirit is to tailor make the spiritual experiences of each sincere Christian believer— conforming us into God's person (hence, conformity as a positive—life changing dynamic).

PRESERVATION

"In order that we—who were the first to hope in Christ— might be for the praise of his glory. And you also were included in Christ when you heard the word of truth, the gospel of salvation—having believed, you were marked in him with a seal, the promised Holy Spirit." (1:12-13)

The original word for seal means to stamp for preservation and security. God knows that the only way to preserve our fragile spiritual state is to do it Himself, through the Holy Spirit. God gives us the privilege of an eternal destiny. Next God preserves it with the Holy Spirit. This preservation occurs through conviction—the radar for sin the Holy Spirit uses in the heart of the believer to avoid the grievous result and development of sin.

INSIGHT

"Who is the deposit guaranteeing our inheritance until the redemption of those who are God's possession--to the praise of his glory." (1:14)

Through this verse we see the description of the purpose of the Holy Spirit. The Holy Spirit is only the deposit of the inheritance of eternal destiny. His Spirit on our spiritual journey is only a part of the insight. Every day

God's Holy Spirit gives us insight to the greater meaning in our lives.

"Insight" is going to be necessary for understanding the truth set out in the book of Ephesians. To gain and grow it will require constant guidance by the Holy Spirit, as well as insight into its meaning coupled with wisdom for application.

The Holy Spirit's work in our lives for conformity, preservation and insight will make the difference in our human struggles and successful spiritual journey.

What do these key words mean to you?

- **CONFORMITY**

- **PRESERVATION**

- **INSIGHT**

Chapter 1

THANKFULNESS

Thankfulness is the first dirty word in this study. Sometimes it becomes a dirty word when we reflect on the holiday that is designed to make us thankful.

Some may try to at least think about being thankful for an hour or so while enjoying a huge feast.

But thankfulness is much more than all this. We could enjoy life so much more if we could analyze and then develop a resourceful model for a thankful spirit.

The lack of a thankful spirit can breed many problems on the human journey. Emotional distress, many mental problems and sometimes even actual physical pain can be a result of the lack of thankfulness. Negative attitudes and pessimism are the most obvious forms when thankfulness is absent. However, a lack of thankfulness can be neatly disguised. The absence of thankfulness can develop many unseen, nameless foes. Problems may arise that develop resentments and bitterness. A lack of thankfulness is dangerous.

The last few verses of chapter one in Ephesians gives us the help we need to compel us to thankfulness, and then to developing a thankful spirit.

COMPELLING FORCES INTO THANKFULNESS

First, to achieve a thankful spirit, one must see the need. 60% of a person's problems could be cured immediately if he was compelled into thankfulness. **60%!?** Usually about 60% of a person's problems have to do with his perception of the situation. A thankful spirit always changes one's perceptions.

Thanksgiving is so much more than just an annual holiday!

As we look at the three compelling forces of thankfulness, we begin to understand why we are sometimes unable to attain the necessary thankful spirit. We need to apply these three compelling forces of thankfulness: recognition, optimism, and care.

Recognition

"For this reason, ever since I heard about your faith in the Lord Jesus and your love for all the saints, I have not stopped giving thanks for you, remembering you in my prayers. I keep asking that the God of our Lord Jesus Christ, the glorious Father, may give you the spirit of wisdom and revelation, so that you may know him better." (1:15-17)

The proclamation—**"that we may <u>know</u> him better"**—instantly sets out our goal and chief motive in the human journey.

It has often been thought that the lessons of life we do not learn in this life, God will teach us in the next. **Knowing Him better** is the greatest concept in the Bible.

Knowing Him better is the highest dimension of the human journey, and scales the heights of spiritual knowledge. This entire Biblical concept is developed from the word *epighosis*, meaning recognition. The recognition of God in life is the zenith of personal experience.

There is help in this compelling force of thankfulness. It is in the form of the Holy Spirit. Two definite words of the Holy Spirit are mentioned--wisdom and revelation. Revelation from the Greek means disclosure; and wisdom is universally known as the ability to take information and make the best directives and decisions from that known information.

To recognize God is to open up the whole spirit of thankfulness. Every Christian believer must allow "knowing Him better" to compel them into a deeper life of thankfulness. At this very point, the Holy Spirit becomes actively involved, as seen in our text.

<u>Optimism</u>

"I pray also that the eyes of your heart may be enlightened in order that you may know the hope to which he has called you, the riches of his glorious inheritance in the saints." (1:18)

The second compelling force of thankfulness is through optimism. Verse 18 shows a remarkably insightful and accurate picture of the need and dynamics of optimism. The Apostle testifies that his prayer is that the "eyes of your heart may be enlightened."

This illustrates the importance of illumination in our lives. We constantly need help with **illumination**—there are many things we miss seeing that are naturally a part of our lives. Pessimism, feeling that nothing ever turns out right, is something we need to see and overcome for successful living.

Pessimism can be as prevalent as unthankfulness. The reason for a negative mindset is due to a definite lack of illumination and hope. Hope, in this text, means to anticipate with unusual pleasure. The difference between a Christian and a non-Christian is optimism. The Christian believer has so much to be optimistic about since the ultimate end of his destiny is the "riches of his glorious inheritance."

The optimism of the Christian believer's spiritual eternal destiny should be enough in itself to compel us into a perpetual spirit of thankfulness.

<u>Care</u>

"And his incomparably great power for us who believe..." (1:19)

Much of our unthankful attitudes come from our excessive concern about our secular lives. The language the Apostle uses for the word power—(dunamis)—is the force of God beyond the normal or ordinary (incomparably). Further, God uses this extraordinary power with magnitude, (greatness), in our lives.

Think about it—if you had the most powerful force in the entire universe as your father—would you be well cared for?

The obvious answer is yes!

God's care for us should greatly compel us to have an enormous spirit of thankfulness.

Recognition, optimism and care should become great compelling forces in the life of the Christian believer toward thankfulness.

The Compelling Forces Toward Thankfulness:

- **RECOGNITION**
- **OPTIMISM**
- **CARE**

DEVELOPING A THANKFUL SPIRIT

There is a plan to develop a thankful spirit. The Apostle gives it to us in an extraordinary way. It is done through the presence of Christ and his relationship to the world.

This should go without saying, but to put us on the right path, the Christian believer must see Christ as the source of all life. Often a mistake has been made--God the Son has been mistakenly considered a smaller part of the Godhead. Not only is Jesus equal, but in ancient cultures, the son of a father was considered as having his own power and **also** the power of the father! Christ must be seen as the source of all life. Four principles can then be applied to develop a thankful spirit.

1. Concentrate continually on the source.

"That power is like the working of his mighty strength, which he exerted in Christ when he raised him from the dead, and seated him at his right hand in the heavenly realms." Ephesians 1:19-20

There is no power greater, including the power exerted at creation, as great as the power of the resurrection which raised Christ Jesus from the dead. The Christian believer must continually concentrate on that power. It is the only way one can begin to develop the thankful spirit that is so necessary.

The idea that Jesus is at the right hand of the Father is especially relevant. We are not concentrating on a dead prophet, but instead our source is a living God. The reason he is at the right hand of the Father is for our intercession—to help us with our needs. Concentration upon Him, our intercessor, helps us to develop a thankful spirit.

2. Submit reverently to the source.

"Far above all rulers and authority, power and dominion, and every title that can be given, not only in the present age but also in the one to come." Ephesians 1:21

We can submit in one of two ways, either of our own free will or against our will, but the truth is—we are going to submit. To willfully submit is to relieve one's self of a great load—a load which normally causes a blockage to a thankful spirit.

3. Obey undeniably the source.

"And God placed all things under his feet and appointed him to be head over everything for the church." Ephesians 1:22

The very basic part of the God-man relationship becomes very clear here: God is God and Jesus is His son—we are under his feet! This goes back to the Garden of Eden and the principle of obedience. God sets the course of creation with definite organization, order, boundaries, roles, and also obedience. The whole problem of the original sin is disobedience. Our constant place must be one of obedience.

The rebellion of the heart which is the result of disobedience is the barrier that must be purged. This is accomplished through a constant state of obedience.

4. Allow completion to the source.

"Which is his body, the fullness of him who fills everything in every way." Ephesians 1:23

This fourth concept in developing a thankful spirit is partially tied to the third concept. Once rebellion is purged through obedience, then the completion of the body can occur. Jesus is the head of the body and we are all parts of the body.

Jesus wants to make us complete. The area of need is the area he completes. He fills "everything in every way." Completion and fulfillment are available as long as the Christian believer is willing. This is a real key in developing a thankful spirit.

Again, it has to be said, that the development of the thankful spirit hinges upon one's personal commitment to the claims of Jesus.

Thankfulness is either a gift of your attitude or a dirty word— which is it for you?

Chapter 2

GRACE

Grace is more than just an important Biblical concept it is a deep and powerful aspect of the human journey.

The problem is many Christian believers don't understand all the implications of grace. Misunderstanding grace is to live far beneath one's privileges as a Christian believer. Because of the lack of its use, grace becomes what we classify as a "dirty word" in the book of Ephesians. Christians just don't seem to realize the full impact of grace.

Grace is primarily a New Testament concept developed from the word "charis," meaning "the divine influence upon the heart and its reflection in life."

"Charis" is really the single most powerful concept in the life of the Christian believer. Ephesians 2:1-10 is our text for the study of grace. From this text, a fairly complete study evolves; complete enough to help to some extent, the Christian believer's entire existence, from the human journey toward his/her spiritual destiny.

The first few verses of chapter 2 show us where we were before grace, with versus 4-7 showing us where we are in grace. Verses 8-10 show us where we are going in grace.

WHERE WE WERE IN GRACE

"As for you, you were dead in your transgressions and sin, in which you used to live when you followed the ways of this world and of the ruler of the kingdom of the air, the Spirit who is now at work in those who are disobedient. All of us also lived among them at one time; gratifying the cravings of our sinful nature and following its desires and thoughts. Like the rest, we were by nature objects of wrath." Ephesians 2:1-3

Many people revel in their "days of old," or as they are more commonly called—"the good old days." It is good to remember our past as long as it is used to emphasize where we are going. The Apostle brings out the past of every person who serves as a necessary reflection for each one of us.

We were dead because of our own sin. It is awesome to consider we were dead—but very necessary to realize! Each of us must reflect often on where we came from. We all came from the same place—death, because of sin. If for no other reason, this exercise of reflection keeps everything in perspective. It is this reflection that gives grace in a life the proper impact it can have.

This second part of where we were in grace shows us a definite place where we should not be.

We used to follow the ways of the world and the ruler of the kingdom of the air. We should **not** be following the ways of the world if we are Christian believers. It is at this point we can show the world where we stand. The Christian believer uses **grace to stand in contrast** to the ways of the world. Without grace there can be no contrast.

Something extra needs to be said about the "prince of the air." This has been commonly held that it is Lucifer. It is too limiting from Paul's inference to say this is Satan only. Prince (archon) in the original text means "first in rank." Air (aer) refers to the unconscious breath or even "realm." This spirit is at work in those who are disobedient. This spirit concept is at work in the unconscious world—in our minds as well as in our world. There is much activity that occurs in the unconscious world. Our heart beats in this realm—every breath we take occurs in this realm. It is a powerful world. Most thought processes and the basis of most decisions are made in this realm. The way **grace** helps us in this very present danger is by helping us be aware, alert and conscious in the world, in our mind and through the "air."

We lived among them at one time, gratifying the cravings of our sinful nature and following its desires and thoughts.

Anyone who claims to be a Christian yet gratifies his/her flesh for the flesh's sake is not a Christian believer. The difference between where we were (gratifying the flesh) and where we are going (following the spirit) is grace. Except for grace, there is no difference between the believer and unbeliever.

> # Anyone who lives to gratify his/her flesh is not a Christian believer!

WHERE WE ARE IN GRACE

"But because of his great love for us, God, who is rich in mercy, made us alive with Christ even when we were dead in transgressions, it is by grace you have been saved. And God raised us up with Christ and seated us with him in the heavenly realms in Christ Jesus in order that in the coming ages he might show the incomparable riches of his grace, expressed in his kindness to us in Christ Jesus." Ephesians 2:4-7

As we allow it, there are several great benefits for the Christian believer from God's grace. "Charis"—"the divine influence upon the heart and its reflection upon life"—is a powerful notion. So it is not surprising that this grace has many great benefits.

Because of grace we are recipients of God's great mercy. We are not going to get what we really deserve. We will never be able to comprehend His mercy. It provides us with all of the necessary spiritual/emotional aspects in our lives:

1. The need to feel needed

2. A sense of belonging

3. A sense of self-worth

4. A sense of destiny

5. A sense of security

The Christian believer need only ask God for mercy to receive the healing, miracle, or touch that one needs.

Because of grace we are made alive. Alive from the Greek text, (zoopoieo), means to revitalize. Christ provides **"the divine influence upon the heart and reflection in life"** to revitalize us. This aliveness or revitalization does not have any boundaries--physical, mental, emotional or spiritual. Whatever the apparent need—the revitalization comes! The only requirement is to yield.

Because of grace we are saved. Saved (sozo), is a word the apostle frequently uses. It is a great word for the expression of deliverance from the sinful nature, as well as protection against perilous dangers of all forms. "Sozo" means to protect and deliver. "The divine influence upon the heart and its reflection in life" brings with it both protection and deliverance.

Because of grace we are endowed with all the rights of Christ. Christ chose to give us his own endowment. An endowment is a structure set up to provide income indefinitely to the one provided for. The work of Christ in redemption is only shadowed by his choice to name us co-beneficiaries with him. We are, because of Christ, joint-heirs of the Father. It is only grace which could do such a work.

Because of grace our future is provided. If we could only see what God is providing for us, it would be far beyond our farthest expectations. Words or pictures or even mental images cannot describe the future we have in store because of grace. Our part in the working of that grace is a walk by faith on a minute by minute, hour by hour, day by day basis. Part of that "seeing by faith" is not fully knowing what our future holds.

WHERE WE ARE GOING IN GRACE

"For it is by grace you have been saved, through faith—and this is not from yourself, it is a gift of God—not by works, so that no one can boast. For we are God's workmanship, created in Christ Jesus to do good works, which God prepared in advance for us to do." Ephesians 2:8-10

The last part of this study on the second dirty word - grace, **the divine influence upon the heart and its reflection in life** - shows us where grace is really taking us. As Christian believers we will see God's grace working in three dynamics - His gift, to His production line, to His preparation process.

Grace takes us to God's gift. Grace takes us to Christ in the first place. All of your unsaved loved ones and friends are brought by God's grace. Far too often we have taken too much responsibility for the condition of someone's soul. The same grace that brought you will bring them.

One day I heard a local pastor tell another person how many people were "saved" last year in their church. There seemed to be a great deal of pride in his voice. Pastors, nor people, ever really get people saved. It is God's gift, His Holy Spirit, His Conviction. We really have only a small part in the total picture—but we do have a responsibility!

Neither, as the text contends, are we ever able to save ourselves. No amount of our own effort can do it. Salvation is a gift by God's grace.

Grace takes us to God's production line. As a Christian believer, you are on God's production line. You are God's workmanship (poiema), or product. As we see ourselves on God's great production line of life, His grace (the divine influence upon the heart and its reflection in life), and His production line become one and the same thing.

Grace takes us up to God's production line. The production line is different, however, from the preparation process.

Grace takes us to God's preparation process. The production line is where we are "put together" and the preparation process is where the "product's" rough edges are filed down. This preparation process happens during the time when the divine influence **reflects in the life** of the Christian believer. As this reflection occurs, the filing down begins. The Christian believer should constantly let grace have its way through all circumstances and situations.

WHERE IS GRACE TAKING YOU TODAY? TOMORROW?

Chapter 3

UNITY

The third dirty word from the book of Ephesians is as intense as any of the rest of the "dirty words."

Unity is a dirty word by virtue of its all too apparent absence in the body of Christ. Fussing, fighting, conflict, gossip and criticism seem to be common place among Christian believers.

Conflict, gossip, and criticism are common because disunity has become an accepted part of "church life." The more it is accepted, the more a stronghold develops. The reasoning has been given that conflict, gossip, and criticism are all normal occurrences because of human nature.

Is human nature an excuse for behavior? Maybe—if you are talking about the human part of the "old man" but certainly not normal for the Christian believer redeemed by Christ and regenerated by the Holy Spirit!

To accept conflict and confusion as normal is to live out of both worlds. It is just not acceptable spiritually. The Holy Spirit and Satan cannot indwell the same vessel.

Unity. That is what God <u>asks - expects - demands</u>! Ephesians 2:11-23 gives us our direction for unity. Verses 11-13 show the awesome scenario of life without unity. This will be a gruesome picture to any child of God who is sincere about personal service to Christ.

29

Verses 14-18 give us some truly good help in our spiritual journey by showing us what are the true "keys to unity." The final verses show us the "result of unity." This should give us a renewing vision and a redeeming commitment to unity in the body of Christ and in the Christian life.

THE HUMAN JOURNEY WITHOUT UNITY

"Therefore, remember that formerly you who are Gentiles by birth and called "uncircumcised" by those who call themselves "the circumcision" (that done in the body by the hands of men)--remember that at that time you were separate from Christ, excluded from citizenship in Israel and foreigners to the covenants of the promise, without hope and without God in the world. But now in Christ Jesus you who once were far away have been brought near through the blood of Christ." Ephesians 2:11-13

Have you ever been on the "outside looking in?" This feeling comes when you want something desperately, but by virtue of fate or destiny, you will never be able to achieve it. This was the apparent lot of the Gentiles. They were separated from spiritual destiny by virtue of their birth. The truth is—this included a large part of the known world. Anyone who is not a Hebrew is a Gentile. Anyone not a Hebrew, once was on the outside looking in on spiritual destiny. But now, through the "blood" of Christ we are—(on the "inside)." The term here for blood is (haima), meaning kindred. All those who are not Hebrews have been adopted by kinship with Christ. We have been unified.

People **don't have to live** lives of confusion, fussing and fighting. As people truly live in unity, they won't live their lives in such darkness and chaos. The text spells out pitfalls should serve as a sort of testing—to determine where one is spiritually. Testing brings a supreme challenge of our spirituality. A test and then a challenge—life without unity is no life at all.

Without Unity we are separate from Christ

Without unity we are totally and completely separate from Christ. Christ is neither in us nor of us when we lack unity. In our day we use the term "Christian" so freely. It has become so common place that we have forgotten what "Christian" means. It means "Christ - like." The likeness of Christ is lived out by "walking as Jesus did." It requires a constant attentiveness to spiritual demands and requirements. It requires unity with God to be a Christian. Without it we are separate from Christ.

The truth is—separation from Christ is just not necessary.

Without Unity we are Excluded v.12

Have you ever been the last one picked for a ball team at school? Have you ever been a guest in a home where you felt or were made to feel like an alien? Without unity, we are excluded from the heavenlies. The alien concept (xenos) is developed here. To see this concept more clearly, picture yourself as one living in a guest house, removed from the main house, never to share meals with the owners, and only given the bare essentials to survive. Daily, you see the palace and the royal family enjoying all the pleasures of life, but being an alien all you will ever be able to do is look. The gospel story of Lazarus and the rich man gives us this picture with upper and lower Hades. Eternity might just be like this.

Without Unity there is no Hope

The term used here for hope, **"elipsis,"** means to anticipate with pleasure. Hope is the dynamic that keeps us going through many of the tough situations of life. Hope is possible only with unity—and unity is possible only with God.

When one does not have unity, the confusion which results is all consuming. One cannot possess any hope if confusion is present.

Without Unity there is no God

God is the one constant in all of life. The most tragic word in the Greek text that the mind could ever consider is "atheos"—without God. Our relationship with God is vital. But then, so is our relationship with others. Unity with God is our submission to uniting my will with His—giving way. Unity with others has to do with uniting with Christian believers for the cause of Christ.

Every personality is different. Conflict develops because one or both of the human personalities will not submit to uniting with one another. Often believers feel like their prayers don't get through. The answer is generally very simple: when one is too stubborn to unite with Christian believers—unity with God is impossible. When walls are built up between people, the wall is built up between them and God as well.

God intends for the Christian believers to be such a team that they operate as one body. This is why we call the church the Body of Christ. Unity is the only way that the team can develop into the Body. The Body has to grow— **to not grow is to die.**

No one can have unity with God without unity with people. That is why local church membership is important. Through uniting with other Christian believers, accountability and responsibility are both possible. Every person needs to have the discipline of accountability, as well as the commitment of responsibility. Every body of Christ or church would benefit by belonging to a denomination. Hence, the church as a unit is accountable and responsible as well. It is good to look at a denominational church with this understanding, as it is popular to be an "independent" church. No church is ever really "independent." A church is always dependent upon Christ, or it is no church. Unity is the critical key to any spiritual relationship. It is so often misunderstood and misapplied, but then that is why we classify it as a dirty word!

WITHOUT UNITY WE ARE:

- **Separated from Christ**
- **Excluded**
- **Hopeless**
- **Without the feeling of God's personal presence**

KEYS TO UNITY

"For he himself is our peace, who has made the two one and has destroyed the barrier, the dividing wall of hostility, by abolishing in his flesh the law with its commandments and regulations. His purpose was to create in himself one new man out of the two, thus making peace, and in this one body to reconcile both of them to God through the cross, by which he put to death their hostility. He came and preached peace to you who were far away and peace to those who were near. For through him we both have access to the Father by one Spirit." Ephesians 2:14-18

The Apostle begins to give us a glimpse of the importance of the **personal spiritual endeavor**. In this text, as well as the one that follows, his personal spiritual journey is likened to building a house or a dwelling place. Through these thoughts, we are given rather intensely, the keys to unity.

Peace

This Greek word for peace, (eirene), means to "join together and hence feel success and prosperity." It is through this peace he has made the two become as one. This passage develops into a graphic description of what peace did--"destroyed the barrier, the dividing wall of hostility." Walls are destroyed because of peace. This specific form of the word "peace" is an important part of unity--"to join together." To make peace with God creates unity. Making peace with others also creates unity. Who do you have walls of hostility built up between? Maybe you are bitter with God. If you are, it is

34

your soul that suffers the most. Many times there are walls of hostility because of manipulation, or selfishness, or wrong motives. These types of behavior create an atmosphere of confusion and hostility. How can you make peace and join together? There are three basic steps involved for this to happen.

1. Realize peace needs to be made. This has to be realized by both parties.

2. Reach common ground. Don't force any issue. Realize that people have to unite for the sake of their souls. It is God's will and plan for people to be in unity with one another.

3. Let people be themselves. People often involve themselves in other people's business. We rob people of necessary personal space. Allowing "personal space" gives a balance to any relationship. We don't need to know everything about everyone. Give people space to express their own personality.

4. Maintain the pace. Everything worthwhile requires constant care. Hot and cold relationships are tragic and unnecessary. Learn to be solid and steady for others.

Abolishment

Abolishment seems like a violent word to use for a key element in unity. It is for abolishment to the flesh. Christ used the abolishment of his flesh to create a new spirituality. He abolished the strict obedience to the law for the strict obedience to himself. The spiritual work of abolishment is the careful work of death to the works of the flesh--all of our "flesh." God creates one man out of two: Christ and me. Together we become a new creation.

Everything done selfishly is a work of the flesh. Everything done out of the will of God is a work of the flesh. Everything done without expressing a spirit of obedience to God is a work of the flesh. To have unity, you have to abolish the flesh.

This is not a "pie in the sky" experience, but a very practical spiritual truth for anyone willing to take that step. For one to have unity, remember, abolishment of the flesh is an imperative. Here are three practical helps in achieving that end:

1. Moderation in all things. The tendency to go overboard is a common manifestation of the flesh. By being moderate, one will develop a definite balance in life. A balanced life is important for the Christian believer.

2. Wait. Our timetable is not always God's timetable. Yield your schedule completely and totally to God.

3. Sensitivity. Listen closely and clearly for God's direction in all things. Be sensitive to your own reactions, emotions, and sensitivities, as well as to those of others.

Reconciliation

Reconciliation is the necessary third key to unity—this is where two people come together and leave as one—two minds become one mind—two bodies have to become one body.

To achieve this goal of total reconciliation, the result must be so complete that it is as though there was no problem in the first place. Often reconciliation becomes a very tedious task which requires hard work. There are four main areas of reconciliation:

1.   Repentance—the actual turning away from previous behavior, which requires a conscious acknowledgment that something has to change. Repentance is accompanied by a commitment that states your willingness to turn from the previous behavior to see the change happen.

2.   Forgiveness—this is an act of the will. You can forgive. For your soul's sake, you must forgive. There are no secrets or magic formulas—just forgive.

3. Restitution—which is often a forgotten point today. Restitution is the total feeling of release from a circumstance or situation. Restitution comes after a process of rehabilitation or reimbursement for a previous behavior. This varies from individual to individual. Sometimes restitution may be just a quiet acknowledgment to self. Restitution may involve things like work, payment, and/or apologies.

4. Restoration—the final component of reconciliation as a key to unity is restoration. Restoration requires coming to the point of mentally and spiritually treating a situation as if it never occurred. Forgiving and forgetting means that the slate is wiped clean and things start over—especially in relationship restoration. Bitterness and resentment need to give way to affirmation and acceptance.

Access

This final key to unity is an often overlooked principle. Access has to do primarily with the maintenance aspect of unity. Christ has provided us with instant access to the Father. Our task is to provide instant access to one another. Access is possible when applying the following suggestions.

1. Communicate clearly. Communication breakdown is 90% of the relationship breakdown. Communication has two requirements—make sure you say what you mean and make sure they understand what you meant. Both of these communication requirements are your responsibility.

2. Careful consideration. When in doubt of someone's actions or motives, make excuses for them. Try to see the other side. Don't cut people off—bring out their thought or their point of view. Don't be afraid to ask them about their point of view.

3. Constant care. People are fragile. All relationships need to be treated like fine china. Take no one or no thing for granted.

Peace, abolishment, reconciliation, access—the keys to unity might take some time, but these four principles are a good start. Apply them carefully as you work toward unity in your life.

THE RESULT OF UNITY

"Consequently, you are no longer foreigners and aliens, but fellow citizens with God's people and members of God's household, built on the foundation of the apostles and prophets, with Christ Jesus himself as the chief cornerstone. In him the whole building is joined together and rises to become a holy temple in the Lord. And in him you too are being built together to become a dwelling in which God lives by his Spirit." Ephesians 2:19-22

The guest who was at one point cut off from the family and could only admire at a distance the inheritance and wealth of the royal family, now becomes a part of that family himself! What a majestic picture! This is exactly what happens as a result of unity. We are no longer strangers and foreigners of God's people—but because of Christ, we are God's people. The concept of fellow citizens becomes so consuming, that the Greek term "sumpolites" means "a native of the same town."

Further, we are not just a grafted branch, or the "runt of the litter," but are given the same foundation of the spiritual family as anyone else. Jesus Christ is the chief cornerstone of our life, with the work of the apostles and prophets having a part of our lives as well. It's instantaneous! We are not required to prove ourselves or required to go through a battery of tests. It is an instant trust because we are spiritually united with God through Christ. We would be much stronger spiritually if we would carry that same spirit to each other—to accept new believers openly, to restore fallen ones quickly, to trust those who profess Christ. Yet, despite what God has done for us in unity through Christ we insist that people go through our subjective battery of criteria to become a part of the body of Christ.

Now we look at the "building." The Apostle refers to our lives as the building. From the original word "oikedome," this word means architecture. There are some very important spiritual, as well as temporal aspects, of the building that is being built.

He is building us to be fitted tightly together. God's structures are never intended to have defects.

His work in our building is carefully organized. From the word (sunarmologeo) we can see that not only is He building a secure building, but He has careful plans. Think about your life as organized by God. Whatever happens—good or bad—it is organized into the building plans by God.

The building is supposed to grow. Verse 22 indicates that "in him you too are being built together." Those experiences which we have are all meant to create growth in us. The application of our experiences is really up to each of us individually, however.

The ultimate destiny of our lives is to become a place where God lives by his Spirit. This is the ultimate goal of the spiritual destiny--to allow the circumstances along the human journey to prepare the immortal soul to be a dwelling place of God throughout eternity. Jesus often said "The Kingdom of heaven is at hand." The dwelling place of God is at hand—it is within the soul.

This is the result of unity in the life of the believer. There sometimes may be "risks" involved, but the dividends of unity are well worth the effort.

---

4 KEYS TO UNITY:
- **Peace**
- **Abolishment**
- **Reconciliation**
- **Access**

Chapter 4

TRUST

How much would we trust the Apostle Paul if he were a modern evangelistic missionary and church leader?

The statements Paul made were so challenging that they must have seemed almost too intense. Even today, through the centuries, his writings have not lost their challenging appeal. They cause our dogmatic ideologies to come crashing down. When confronted head to head with scriptural truth we have no other recourse, except to **trust.**

Yet, we have been terribly disappointed in people. We have trusted before only to be let down. We have become suspicious of everyone. This is why "trust" is our fourth dirty word.

How do we -- who can we -- trust?

How do we develop trust in ourselves?

These are questions Ephesians 3:1-13 answer. These are appropriate questions in our day of child abuse, political scams, bribery and corruption in high places, marital unfaithfulness, television evangelists, and day to day untruths. The Apostle helps us see that we can know for sure!

Who Do We Trust?

"For this reason I, Paul, the prisoner of Christ Jesus for the sake of you Gentiles—surely you have heard about the administration of God's grace that was given to me for you, that is, the mystery made known to me by Revelation, as I have already written briefly. In reading this then, you will be able to understand my insight into the mystery of Christ, which was not made known to men in other generations as it has now been revealed by the Spirit to God's holy apostles and prophets. This mystery is that through the gospel the Gentiles are heirs together with Israel, members together of one body, and sharers together in the promise in Christ Jesus." Ephesians 3:1-6

There doesn't seem to be a balance as far as trust is concerned. We either trust too much and get hurt or too little and don't give the right people a chance. There are some guidelines for trust. There are times when these guidelines are not foolproof—especially with those who are careful manipulators and great deceivers. But then, we end up knowing who these manipulators and deceivers are anyway.

The testimony of the Apostle is our criteria for the development of these principles. When Paul's teachings are executed properly, they will provide some healthy guidelines for trust. By doing so, trust will rise above being just another of the dirty words of our society.

1. Trust someone who is responsible in their area of responsibility.

A person's so called "track record" is very, very important. The track record is relevant only in their area of expertise. Have they been faithful and committed to their area or not? Many times people get too involved in areas other than their area of expertise. It is in this way many people become untrustworthy. When people venture out into other areas they often are unsuccessful. The real test is to go back to the person's area of expertise and see if they have been proven responsible.

The Apostle's responsibility was the "administration of God's grace." Administration is similar to the administration of a household or estate—a spelled-out set of responsibilities. Was Paul responsible in it? Yes. Then he can be trusted.

If the Apostle decided to do surgery instead of his well-known side occupation of tent making—he couldn't be trusted. If he did surgery, it would not be his area of responsibility. But he could still be trusted in preaching as long as he remains responsible in preaching. The error that is often made occurs when people do something out of their realm of responsibility—and then we don't trust them in <u>any area, any more</u>. Learn to distinguish these areas from one another.

2. Trust someone when they are accountable for what they say.

As a child I use to go with my grandfather up to the car garage every morning about 10 a.m. In that town of 200 people total, a bunch of them met up at the garage to loaf. During their time together they would share various opinions on a wide range of topics. No one really had any education on what they said, nor accountability for what they expounded. They could lie, start rumors, and manipulate one another with no accountability. The rather vivid point is—none of them could be trusted— because none of us was accountable.

Do you realize we are held accountable for every word we utter? The Christian believer is accountable. In addition, if you work a job you are accountable to your employer. A student is accountable to his teacher. A husband and wife are accountable to each other. A child is accountable to a parent. The church member is accountable to the church. Every Christian is accountable to God. Accountability is necessary. Don't trust anyone who is not accountable for what he says or what he does.

The Apostle was given revelation by God. He was accountable to God for the information he gave others. He was also accountable to fellow Christian believers.

3. Trust someone when you can understand them.

Don't trust something blindly that you cannot understand. Ask questions, be specific—seek understanding. Many times confusion has resulted because a person didn't understand a sales pitch, a fund drive, a Sunday school lesson, a special offering, or a sermon.

The truth is—it takes God's help to understand the mystery of Christ. This mystery of Christ has great ramifications into eternity and we must understand it to trust it. The only way we can trust the gospel is by the help of the Spirit.

A caution should be given here—just because something is not understandable, it should not make one acutely suspicious, but should cause one to pursue understanding. If it is not understandable to you after sufficiently trying to understand, don't trust it/them.

The pursuit of understanding needs to be life long. There is a condition of trust which needs to occur to understand something. In a way, as the understanding grows--trust should also grow. No amount of trust ever comes "presto."

Another caution with understanding someone is in the area of presentation. You may not understand something because of how it is presented. The more you hear similar presentations—the better you understand—only because you get use to how it is presented. Be careful to not get too suspicious too quickly.

4. Trust someone when the Spirit bears witness.

"Revealed by the Spirit" is a well-known concept of the Apostle. He truly believed in the working of the Holy Spirit in the lives of people. The same is true today. All of the hidden things in life can be "revealed by the Spirit." Originally, the word "revealed" (apokalupto) means to "take the cover off."

Are you wondering if this situation or that one can be trusted? Ask the Holy Spirit to "take the cover off." Are you wondering if this person or that one can be trusted? Ask the Holy Spirit to "take the cover off" for you to see. This is the work of the Holy Spirit, in your life, as you become filled with Him. The Holy Spirit within you has the capacity to bear witness with the Spirit within others. If the Spirit is good, then trust it. If you feel a Spirit which is not so positive—be careful—find out more.

5. Trust someone when they speak the truth.

Truth can always be trusted. If the person speaking is speaking the truth, they can be trusted for the truth they speak. This is not to say they can be trusted blindly, but having a capacity to speak the truth is sure a great start. If people speak the truth one time, they are bound to speak the truth again!

The Apostle uses a very graphic illustration of truth: The Jews are God's chosen people—then he reached out to the Gentiles. Now we are heirs together. We share together in the promise of Christ Jesus.

Pride can often stand in the way of truth. But truth is the absolute—the bottom line. Unless we trust God's promises, commands, and order, we will not have truth. We have to trust truth.

Developing Trust

"I became a servant of this Gospel by the gift of God's grace given me through the working of his power. Although I am less than the least of all God's people, this grace was given me: to preach to the Gentiles the unsearchable riches of Christ, and to make plain to everyone the administration of this mystery, which for ages past was kept hidden in God who created all things. His intent was that now, through the church, the manifold wisdom of God should be made known to the rulers and authorities in the heavenly realms, according to his eternal purpose which he accomplished in Christ Jesus our Lord. In him through faith in him we may approach God with freedom and confidence. I ask you, therefore not to be discouraged because of my sufferings for you, which are your glory." Ephesians 3:1-13

From time to time we all need to be trusted. Often we need to be trusted quicker than we are able to develop trust. Developing trust requires sincerity and hard work. Trust is everything in human relationships. Our text shows us 4 to 5 ways of developing trust. These are principles for spiritual purposes--not for selfish ones. We must never forget to differentiate between the spiritual and the selfish reasons. To develop trust for Scripture, it must be done with spiritual purposes.

"LET HIS POWER WORK IN YOU"

The sign of the sincere Christian believer is the fruit of the Spirit working with efficiency and might in a life. This is "His power working in you." The result of His power working in you is trust. God working in a life creates great trust because of the obvious change in a person.

Is the power of God obvious in your life? The most apparent way to tell is if your walk and your talk match. Hypocrites who say one thing and do another cannot be trusted. Be a real person. Be honest with yourself and be honest with others.

"DIE TO YOUR OWN DESIRE"

Society tells us to strive, covet, drive and desire. The Apostle gives us the model for the humility of the child of God. "I am less than the least of all God's people." Paul had died to his own desire, to his own motives. Death to one's own desire brings the vision of God's dream to us. The result of what happens is clearly illustrated in the text: "this grace was given to me--to preach to the Gentiles the unsearchable riches of Christ..."

47

Why do we hold on to our own desires? Generally because we like to figure it all out--we like to be in control. The old nature within us has appetites that ache to be fed. It is the old carnal man which causes all this fuss. We have to overcome this carnal man by death to Him. Not until one dies, does one even truly live.

"MAKE IT PLAIN WHAT YOU STAND FOR"

Don't be "two-faced." People trust someone who clearly stands for something rather than those who don't stand for anything.

By making it "plain," be consistent. Don't loudly espouse how you feel, but quietly and firmly stand up for what you believe in. If you do this, people will respect you for who you are, as well as respect you for what you stand for.

"BE A TEAM PLAYER FOR ETERNITY"

Enjoy every day...for life is for growth, for expectation, but mostly for the opportunity to be a player on God's team.

God's team doesn't just end when we pass through the tunnel from this life to the next, but goes on past this life. God is building a team for the future. We are now just trying out for the team. Are you, right now, making God's team? Even after you make the team, there will be constant training and trial. See yourself as a team player for eternity. If you do this, then trust will come easy for others. People will see more in your life than temporary pleasure and quick fixes. You will be trustworthy, not just in a temporary way, but forever.

"DON'T BE HOT AND COLD OR UP AND DOWN"

The least trustworthy person is one who is up and down or hot and cold. People need evidence of consistency to enable them to trust. If you feel like you are not trusted, then discover if you have been inconsistent in any area. Here are some tips for staying steady:

1. Reach a comfortable balance in all areas of your life.

2. Practice moderation in all things. The ones who go overboard are never trusted.

3. Prove yourself to others by being yourself.

4. Express your needs clearly to others.

5. Discover if there is some reason that you are not steady. If it is something from your past, then correct it.

Becoming trustworthy may require time and effort, but don't let that discourage you. Trust does not have to be a dirty word--in either area, gaining or giving trust.

> **Only those who learn to trust are those who should be trusted!**

Chapter 5

GROWTH

The fifth dirty word in the book of Ephesians is **growth**. It has become a dirty word through the seemingly vast amount of Christian believers who feel they have arrived. Because of the attitude of self satisfaction, the lack of growth has become a spiritual problem of epidemic proportion.

How does it happen?

The dirty word "growth" starts as an evil form of deception which makes one feel that they have mastered the aspects of scripture—they have become a self appointed Bible scholar. To contrast, growth is a vital part of the human journey, even developing our spiritual destiny. God's commission to Adam was: "Go forth and replenish the earth," which illustrates growth cycles.

The major reason for growth stagnation in the life of the Christian believer still seems to be a lack of interest in God's word. When I think of just some of the things contained in God's Word I have to conclude that it must take a lot of work not to grow!

Here are some ways to growth through God's Word: the Ten Commandments; fifty ways to please God; principles for good family relationships; guidelines for church leaders; the unconditional promises; promises about the future, prosperity, and spiritual blessings; warnings concerning nations; promises to the individual; proverbs concerning God; proverbs concerning eternal life;

proverbs concerning stewardship; proverbs concerning witnessing; facts about the Holy Spirit; animals God used miraculously; supernatural journeys; Old Testament prophecies fulfilled by Jesus; twenty encounters with angels; 25 ways Old Testament heroes exercised faith; rules concerning conduct of sex; characteristics of non-Christians in the last days; complete teachings on love; the gifts of the Holy Spirit; the fruits of the Holy Spirit; the facts about sin; the facts about Satan; all the miracles of the Bible; and descriptions of the Kingdom of Heaven.

The truth is—IT TAKES A LOT OF EFFORT NOT TO GROW!

Ephesians 3:14-22 gives us the ten areas in which every Christian believer needs to grow. These growth areas are not all inclusive, but they certainly provide ten areas whereby one can grow in any other area(s) necessary through simply applying these ten.

"For this reason I kneel before the Father, from whom his whole family in heaven and on earth derives its name. I pray that out of his glorious riches He may strengthen you with power through His Spirit in your inner being, so that Christ may dwell in your hearts through faith. And I pray that you, being rooted and established in love, may have power, together with all the saints, to grasp how wide and long and high and deep is the love of Christ, and to know this love that surpasses knowledge--that you may be filled to the measure of all the fullness of God. Now to Him who is able to do immeasurably more than all we ask or imagine, according to his power that is at work within us, to Him be glory in the church and in Christ Jesus throughout all generations for ever and ever! Amen!" Ephesians 3:14-21

SURRENDER

"For this reason I kneel before the Father..."

To kneel or bow is an interesting concept. It is the word "kampto" meaning the "act of bending." Bending at the knee is an ancient act of surrender, and indicates an ultimate part in spiritual initiative.

Surrendering is the pinnacle in growth if it is done systematically. The Christian believer would be wise to make surrendering a "first thing in the morning" habit. Yielding and submitting to God's every direction in a day's time is a scenario of growth which is untapped in its impact on the life of the Christian believer.

Surrendering is the ultimate in growth if it is also done spontaneously, as in a moment by moment experience as needed throughout the day. When things are frustrating, surrender it to God. When things are disappointing, surrender it to God. When things are discouraging, surrender it to God. When you fail, surrender it to God.

Surrendering is the ultimate in growth if it is done effectively. Effective surrender is a three-fold process:

1. See your source of everything as coming from God. Everything begins and ends with God.

2. See your source of help coming from God. This makes it clear that everything you need comes from God.

3. See the source of what you need as only having one option--surrendering to God!

Surrender systematically, spontaneously, and effectively.

IMAGE

"...the Father from whom his whole family in heaven and on earth derives its name."

"And God said, Let us make man in our image, after our likeness..." Genesis 1:26

"So God created man in his own image..." Genesis 1:27

Image is a powerful Hebrew concept "tselem" meaning to shade to resemble. This concept in Genesis 1 means more than just an event, but a continuation of the process of becoming "more and more like."

The Ephesians text presents us with the second area of growth for the Christian believer. This area of the image of God comes from the fact that we are part of the family of God. It is clear that we are named after the Father. The Christian believer derives his/her name from the Father. We are family. As family there are three truths of this heavenly family life we must consider.

1. If God is your Father you naturally will look like Him. The fall from grace in the garden made us all estranged. Although we may resemble Him, the resemblance is very vague. It takes time with God to bring His features out in you. Although this does not always hold true, it is humorous to note how pets, especially dogs, look like their masters. The resemblance comes through the amount of time spent with each other.

2. If God is your Father you will act like Him. You may never look completely like Him until heaven, but you

53

can at least always act like Him, since it is just an act of the will.

3. If God is your Father you will seek His counsel. Finding out what His will is and what His wishes are, is important because He is your Father.

VIGOR

"I pray that out of his glorious riches he may strengthen you with power through his spirit in your inner being."

Most Christian believers testify to feeling like they are either overworked, over scheduled, burned out, or in retirement as far as their Christian service is concerned.

Seemingly more and more people want less and less to do, with no recruits waiting in the wings anxiously anticipating something to do. The problem is vigor. We don't have the vigor we once did.

I have carefully analyzed why we have lost vigor. The old "store your treasures in heaven" routine is not working. Neither is "Jesus could come back today!" While these old motivating story lines might have done the job in the past, it doesn't seem to be doing it today. We need vigor! Christian believers need to be challenged that an area of growth for each of them must be vigor.

An older concept of vigor is unction. With this term, a light might have come on for older Christians. It is the under 40 age group, who may not have heard of the term. "Strengthen (krataioo) the inner (eti) man (anthropos)" is an important New Testament concept. Strengthen means "increase with vigor" your inner man or countenance. The Biblical imperative appears to be <u>God wants us to</u>

grow in the increasing of our vigor on a continuing basis, and it should be reflected in our countenance! Christian believer--how is your vigor?

Where do we start!?!

First, realize that the only thing in this life you take with you is what you have done for Christ.

Secondly, determine to do only those things for Christ which He has gifted you.

Third, if you feel a loss of Christian victory or loss of victorious Christian living, then seek God to strengthen the inner man.

Fourth, put aside all preconceived notions or prejudices. Simply, find freedom with spiritual vigor.

Finally, allow vigor to be a continuing spiritual experience.

CONVICTION

"So that Christ may dwell in your hearts through faith."

Conviction is a dearly beloved friend to the Christian believer. Without conviction, we have no growth. Every Christian believer should sincerely seek the conviction of the Holy Spirit after every episode of a spiritual challenge with two very important questions as they are asked through the believer's heart:

Holy Spirit, what is it you are saying to me?

Holy Spirit, are there some things that need to be changed within me?

The penetrating truth comes into play in the text through three concepts:

1. **Dwell—(katoikeo)—to house permanently**

2. **Heart—(kardia)—thoughts or feelings**

3. **Faith—(pistis)—this context means "conviction."**

According to the text conviction is in essence the dwelling place of Christ. Interpreted loosely the text would say—so that Christ may be housed permanently in your thoughts and feelings through conviction.

Conviction, then, needs to be housed permanently in the thoughts and feelings of the Christian believer. And once conviction is housed, it must grow. Not only is the Christian believer to house conviction, and allow it to grow, but should continually see it as the beloved friend we mentioned!

BENEVOLENCE

"And I pray that you, being rooted and established in love."

Ask 150 people what love is and you will receive 150 (or more) definitions of that love is. Often we think in terms of romance or "mush-mush." To the Christian believer, love must be rooted and grounded, and the believer himself must be rooted and grounded in love. To the

Christian believer, love must be simple benevolence or giving.

There are two truths about benevolence that are seen in the text:

Giving must be rooted. The Greek word (rhizo) or rooted means to be stable. Giving must be steady and stable, while the person himself must be steady and stable.

Giving must be growing, constantly under construction. "Established" (themelioo), comes from the word which means to lay a basis for a building, and then erect it by consolidation.

We need to be <u>STABLE</u> and <u>GROWING</u>. There are really no hard and fast rules concerning giving, except these two. It is good for the Christian believer that there are only two to be concerned about! But each believer must commit to steady and growing giving!

A common mistake made in the Christian life is the mentality which believers we have done "our share." The Christian believer must grow and continue to move past this deception of the faith. Our giving must be steady and growing, not unsteady, unpredictable or faltering.

KNOWLEDGE

"May have power, together with all the saints, to grasp how wide and long and high and deep is the love of Christ, and to know this love that surpasses knowledge."

This journey called the Christian life is a constant learning experience. It continues to grow on and on. The

Christian life has always been assumed that the pursuit of knowledge will continue on throughout all of eternity. Knowledge, in general, is an important area in which every Christian believer needs to grow. Knowledge of all kinds is indeed a great benefit of the faith. To learn is vital in growing and staying fresh.

This picture of knowledge is a vivid one. We see four specific dimensions of the pursuit of knowledge. They all conclude with the fact that love surpasses all of knowledge. Of such is the total picture of knowledge. The four dimensions of this journey in the knowledge of the love of Christ are breadth, length, depth and height.

BREADTH, (platos), means spread out flat. Breadth is an interesting concept that the journey of growing holds before us. We are apparently giving an invitation to this journey in knowledge of Christ—and it is spread out flat before us.

LENGTH, (mekos), means big. The pursuit of knowledge is a BIG journey, one in which no one should get bored.

DEPTH, (bathos), is translated to mean extent. The journey of knowledge is quite extensive. It is certainly far deeper than just education, but delves deeply into wisdom, discernment, talent, graces and gifts, etc.

HEIGHT, (unpsos) or elevation, indicates that our growth in knowledge is far higher than just this life, but goes on deeply into eternity.

Every Christian believer must commit himself to being a life long learner!

BALANCE

"That you may be filled to the measure all the fullness of God."

Normally, it does not take much to get out of balance. Christian believers tend to be out of balance often, either by going overboard on a task or under doing a task.

When tires get a certain amount of mileage on them, they have to be balanced. They are taken to the computer and weights adjusted. Then back on the road. Christians need to be like that.

Balance, in our lives, needs to grow—it has to. To become effective, the Christian believer needs to have a more delicate and ever increasing finer-tuned balance. "Growth of Balance" may be a unique concept, but I see it obviously illustrated from two words in the text: filled (pleroo) and fullness (plezoma).

The term filled can best be understood as "cramming a net full." To the Hebrew a net crammed full of fish was the hallmark of abundance. It should not be surprising to the Christian believer that this was the Apostle's prayer. This should be our prayer for one another!

Even if the physical or material net of the Christian believer is not crammed full of fish, at least the spiritual net should be.

Yet, being "filled" can make one go out of balance. That is where the importance of this second term "fullness" comes in.

Fullness could best be interpreted "to complete being filled." Here is how we can properly view this whole scene: first of all, God wants your nets to be crammed full of fish. When they are—how are you going to have the strength to pull several tons of fish on to the shore? This is where one could become unbalanced. But God can intercede with "fullness," the appropriate gifts and graces and strength to do what it takes to care for the net full of fish. Not only does God give a blessing, but gives the Christian believer whatever it takes to handle the blessing. We can see God's divine balance that He wants to grow inside every Christian believer.

Every effort must be made in our modern world for the Christian believer to remain balanced. Unbalanced "believers" lose the race--we miss our objectives. There is no reason for imbalance to happen. We must have both the "filled" and the "fullness."

VISION

"Now to him who is able to do immeasurably more than all we ask or imagine."

The vision of the Christian believer should be in a constant state of growth. God is able—and our vision is tied to God. Beyond that, he can do more than we could ever ask him to do, or even imagine him doing.

"Vision" is our ability to formulate, in our meager way, the abilities of God's work through me. The ability of God's work through me is immeasurably more than all we ask or could imagine.

How do we allow our vision to grow?

1. Every vision must be God-centered.

2. Every vision must have something to do with the intercession of needs for others.

3. Every vision must build upon and be greater in scope than the previous one.

Let your vision grow!

POWER

"According to his power"

Power is simply a force. The force of God must grow. It must grow in the life of the Christian believer, as well as outside the life of the Christian believer. The power of God is not something mystical. It is a fact of creation. It grows by the exercise of three things:

1. Believe the power of God is at work everywhere.

2. Believe that there is no life except for the power of God.

3. Believe that the more the power of God is exercised by faith, the greater the power of God becomes.

EFFICIENCY

"That is at work within us..."

Efficiency could be better thought of as Christian excellence. Work, (energio), means to be more active and efficient.

The work we do in all areas of life needs to get better and better to the glory of God, which is why it is called the growth of efficiency.

The concept of efficiency must become a mentality and infiltrate the work places of the Christian believer. Wherever a Christian believer is, there must be Christian excellence. Our capacity to do quality work could lead more people to Christ than any number of sermons.

This concept of efficiency must also infiltrate the church. The church is still a volunteer organization, but just because one is not paid for services, it should not hurt the quality of one's work. In fact, because we are doing something for Christ's sake, that should compel and motivate us to do better than our best. He gave everything for us!

This concept of efficiency must also infiltrate the home and every personal project, too. We must not slough off in quiet or personal moments. Christian excellence must be our lifestyle and mentality.

Grow. Get use to it. God intends for us to grow. His will is that we grow. And somehow, some way, He will see to it that we will grow!

The Components of "Growth" that make it a "Dirty Word:"

- Surrender
- Image
- Vigor
- Conviction
- Benevolence
- Knowledge
- Balance
- Vision
- Power
- Efficiency

Chapter 6

CONSISTENCY

The sixth dirty word in the book of Ephesians can be summed up from 4:16, "From him the whole body joined and held together by every supporting ligament, grows, and builds itself up in love, as each part does its work."

Consistency is more than just doing something constantly; it is being steady and strong in an area. Consistency is like the steady application of pressure to a wound. Ephesians 4:1-16 gives us the help we need for consistency.

Consistency is a dirty word because of the obvious problem which most Christian believers have. Many believers are either hot or cold, or on again and off again. This kind of behavior is not God's will. God's plan for us is one of steadiness.

This is a fairly complete study in consistency. Part 1, verses 1-7 shows us the elements of consistency. Part 2, verses 9-13 show us the principles of consistency. The last part, verses 14-16 shows us a conclusion of consistency. With even a small part of openness to Scripture, the Christian believer can find the help and strength one needs to be the believer God wants us to be.

The Elements of Consistency

"As a prisoner for the Lord, then, I urge you to live a life worthy of the calling you have received. Be completely humble and gentle; be patient, bearing with one another in love. Make every effort to keep the unity of the Spirit through the bond of peace. There is one body and one spirit—just as you were called to one hope when you were called—one body, one faith, one baptism; one God and Father of all, who is over all and through all and in all. But to each one of us grace has been given as Christ apportioned it. This is why it says: "When he ascended on high, he led captives in his train and gave gifts to men." Ephesians 4:1-8

Do you care about your Christian journey at all?

If you do, then you care about the elements of consistency. If you don't care about your Christian journey it will be evident through your consistency.

Each of us needs definite direction and help. Chapter 4:1-7 gives us six elements of consistency, which relate to the character of each of us.

The Apostle says, "<u>I urge you to live a life worthy of the calling you have received.</u>" By his intensity you can see that our lives are worth some preservation. Further, our lives are worth some worthiness, but only because of our calling. Do you realize that God calls us to salvation? We have received the calling of eternal life. To "live up" to this calling requires the careful execution of six elements of consistency--which need to be done consistently!

Appreciation for others. The opposite of the appreciation of others is taking them for granted. An appreciation for others is motivated by consistency, and consistency in turn is motivated by an appreciation for others.

The appreciation concept comes from the Greek text, "tapeinophresune," meaning "completely humble," meaning the humiliation of the mind. This gives us the depiction that we must remove arrogance from our lives.

We tend toward arrogance far too often, especially when we wrap ourselves up in our own accomplishments or status. When we get "into self" the arrogant spirit grows and thrives within us. Along with arrogance, inconsistency develops. Families grossly develop arrogance at times, looking down on other families, making fun of others, and becoming condescending to other families. This type of behavior and mindset creates inconsistency. The humility referred to in the text means that mentally we view ourselves as "becoming the same."

We should raise our families to see equally, not arrogantly. If we don't want Billy to play with Johnny, change Billy's play time; don't make Billy out to be better than Johnny.

Another area of special attention in appreciating others is—never take people for granted. In any setting, we take strong, consistent people for granted. This is tragic, because as we do take others for granted we are the ones who become inconsistent. We become dependent on the consistent ones, and then become personally weak. It happens in marriage, in families, in work places, and in churches. We lean on the strong ones, take them for granted, and then become inconsistent in the process.

Appreciation for others requires constant and diligent effort...and by doing so develops consistency.

Understanding. Most inconsistency can be traced back to a time and place. Usually we can trace anything back to because of this—or that—or because "they" said this or that. Further, when this episode happened it is generally because of a misunderstanding, a communication breakdown. This breakdown requires what the text calls "gentleness."

Gentleness is applied in the 21st century through a spirit of understanding:

- **Make excuses for people.**

- **Don't wear your feelings on your sleeve.**

Your consistent Christian journey is at stake here.

Endurance. There are times that you are just not going to feel like being consistent. The reasons will be varied, and some even justified. Endurance must kick in when consistency wants to end.

There are really no deep secrets about endurance, just simple fortitude. "Patience" is the scriptural concept for this. In today's society, we just don't take patience far enough on into endurance.

Loyalty. Another element of consistency is loyalty, taken from "bearing with one another." Loyalty is really endurance in human relationships. Our loyalty to people must be deep and lasting. Yet today because of petty differences, we are ready to turn on one another. The only way to develop consistency is by being loyal to one another.

There are many temptations in the human relationships to become disloyal. We should always make an assumption that loyalty will be present. We should never have to say "This is just between you and me." Confidentiality is the fruit of loyalty.

We should never have to mention that loyalty is necessary. Loyalty should be the basis for every relationship.

Invisibility. To be consistent, you have to be invisible. You can't be desirous of recognition or reward. If you are, it will become a motivating force to your behavior. When that happens, you will only be consistent based on your reward--that is not consistency at all.

The concept used in this passage of unity, (hevotes), projects the thought of invisibility. Don't do things to be seen or noticed or recognized. Do it for the glory of God. This is the only way to maintain consistency.

Linking Together. This final element in this study of consistency comes from the "bond of peace." We need to link together for purposes of accountability. Accountability provides the Christian believer with the necessary boundaries of submission and service that one needs. Without accountability, there is independence, which is the breeding ground for rebellion.

Most every group we can belong to provides accountability. That is the reason for belonging to the group. Yielding oneself to the principles of the group is good for the character, especially in the areas of commitment. "Linking together" is the concept for providing this to us. We must link together with others in this area of accountability and consistency.

These elements of consistency may not be new, or all-inclusive, but it is about six areas which can change our lives for the better--because consistency is our friend!

The Work of Consistency

"(What does 'he ascended' mean except that he also descended to the lower earthly regions. He who descended is the very one who ascended higher than all the heavens, in order to fill the whole universe.) It was he who gave some to be apostles, some to be prophets, some to be evangelists, and some to be pastors and teachers, to prepare God's people for works of service, so that the body of Christ may be built up until we all reach unity in the faith and in the knowledge of the son of God and become mature, attaining to the whole measure of the fullness of Christ." Ephesians 4:9-13

The work of consistency is two-dimensional. The first dimension is the development of consistency within the Christian believer. The second dimension is the work consistency has upon consistency, or you have to consistently be consistent.

There are six principles found in the text for the work of consistency in the life of the Christian believer--completion, build up, unity, recognition, maturity and strength.

The first work is **completion**. In the text, as "words of service," we can never be complete until we are consistent. Among the works of service mentioned are those ministries for what God uses the Christian believers. Think of the system God has devised for the church—next consider how often our lack of consistency has hurt the plan of God for people. When we are ready, they are not. When they are ready, we are not. Our lack of consistency must grieve the Holy Spirit. To see this work of completion accomplished, everyone must execute the work of service God has for each of us. When only part of the team is doing part of the work, God's plan cannot be accomplished. It is only when we are consistent we become complete—and it is only when we are complete, that we can be truly consistent.

The Apostle uses the concept "oikodome," that he has already used four times. This time it is used for the work of consistency: **Build up** the foundation and building of a structure. In this instance, Paul wants the Body of Christ to be built up. God wants to build up everyone—all of creation!

It is only through consistency that we can build up the body of Christ. The body of Christ can never be built up through an on again/off again spiritual existence. The bottom line of "built up" is consistency, and consistency is the bottom line of build up!

Thirdly, when people are in **unity** they are going and pulling in the same direction. Unity can only happen through consistency. People pull together in proportion to their trust in the consistency of one another!

"Reach the knowledge of the Son of God," is the fourth concept (epignosis), which means **recognition**. To recognize the Son of God is to make him an interwoven part of our lives on a moment by moment basis. Contemporary Christianity has lost the power of Jesus. We develop programs, self-help programs and ministries, but where is Jesus? Jesus made it very plain--"I am the way, the truth and the life. No one can come to the

Father, but through me!" Jesus is not just an option--he is the only way to consistency. Jesus today, Jesus tomorrow, Jesus always! This is the concept of Jesus recognition.

It is important that every Christian believer make application of this. Sometimes we have been Christians so long that we have forgotten about Jesus. Somehow our eyes get off Jesus and on to people. The next thing that occurs is our own inconsistency. Jesus is consistency—and consistency shows Jesus.

The scriptural concept of **maturity** (teleios) generally means complete. This concept is expanded in the NIV with "perfect man" illustrating that consistency develops maturity. Simply, as we are consistent, a "sticking with it," rather than "giving up," creates maturity.

Young people often dismiss the idea of "sticking with it" as old fashioned. The truth is "sticking with it" shows maturity. Maturity is consistency, and consistency is mature!

"Attaining the full measure of perfection," has the greatest impact of all the works of consistency. Consistency creates and multiplies **strength**.

Consistency is like a muscle, when it is exercised it becomes stronger. When it is not used, it goes flabby. When consistency is exercised, and then forgotten, it is useless.

Consistency in any area will strengthen that whole area. If there is an area of need—being consistent will allow a person find a way to meet the need. Whatever the area, if one tries to redeem himself in a steady and consistent manner, the desired result will come to pass. If we fail at the works of consistency, we fail at the entire Christian journey.

The Results of Consistency

"Then we will no longer be infants, tossed back and forth by the waves, and blown here and there by every wind of teaching and by the cunning and craftiness of men in their deceitful scheming. Instead, speaking the truth in love, we will in all things grow up into him who is the Head, that is, Christ. From him the whole body, joined and held together by every supporting ligament, grows and builds itself up in love, as each part does its work." Ephesians 4:14-16

The text beautifully illustrates for us the result of consistency. God's will for the Christian believer is seen in verse 16, "from him the whole body joined and held together by every supporting ligament grows and builds itself up in love, as each part does its work."

The Apostle illustrates the five pitfalls we are to avoid, which are brought about by inconsistency. Then he concluded with the two great results of consistency. Concluding these thoughts, Paul then writes of the body of Christ and illustrates to each of us that we are part of the body. We are joined with one another. We are held together to one another. We grow up with one another. We build up one another. But it all happens only through consistency. As we see this happen in the church, it is only happening because it is clearly happening in ourselves. However, the admonition is to avoid five things:

No longer be infants (nepios), or simple-minded. Even more strongly, "nepios" means don't be spoon-fed. Inconsistency is a sign of a baby.

Tossed back and forth, meaning to surge and fluctuate. This is exactly what the inconsistent person does. He is tossed around by his own lack of fortitude.

Blown here and there. Inconsistent people are carried around by what suits them at the time. They might put all their energy into one program for now, but before it is completed, they give it up and try something else.

Every wind of teaching is to follow what is popular at the time, whether that be seed faith, financial success, marriage and family, second coming, etc. They don't have the courage to stay with anything and swallow any new teaching that comes by.

Finally, don't follow **deceitful scheming**, or from the Greek "plane," the fraudulent. Inconsistent people follow the fraudulent, and fraudulence is a common fruit of inconsistency. Primarily, fraudulence is due to the fact that inconsistency always requires cover-ups.

We can see the two main results of consistency--truth and growth.

Inconsistency is a lie, and consistency is the truth. You can count on a consistent person.

Growth, (auxemo), means to wax larger. Consistency creates growth--steady and strong growth.

Chapter 7

HONESTY

On the farm there are gates. Every fence must have at least one gate because from time to time, every farmer must go in or out of the pasture for some reason or another. Without a gate, the fence would be useless because there would be no way to let the animals in. Gates allow the farmer to tend to the needs of the animals. Gates have to be watched. After passing through the gate it takes a little effort to make sure it is closed again. If left open, all the animals will leave the pasture.

Honesty is the gate of the human endeavor. Honesty is the gateway through which we all must pass. However, honesty has become a dirty word in our society. In fact, people seem to work extremely hard at trying to avoid honesty, or to get by with just the minimum requirements.

There are three dimensions of honesty; honesty with self, honesty in application, and honesty in life. These three dimensions can become a program to a better life. The basic reason why people cannot find help for themselves is because of a lack of honesty. To develop honesty, we must make careful adjustments in areas of need. The text, and our study of honesty, will present us with these necessary possible adjustments. Look and live!

HONESTY WITH SELF

"So I tell you this, and insist on it in the Lord, that you must no longer live as the Gentiles do in the futility of their thinking. They are darkened in their understanding and separated from the life of God because of the ignorance that is in them due to the hardening of their hearts. Having lost all sensitivity, they have given themselves over to sensuality so as to indulge in every kind of impurity with a continual lust for more." Ephesians 4:17-19

"To indulge in every kind of impurity..." doesn't that sound terrible? But it continues..."with a continual lust for more." There is absolutely nothing in this world that ever really satisfies. Many people are searching. Their search is for something real, something that will satisfy. Generally they end up trying any number of things which are cheap substitutes and fakes which only last a short time.

Honesty, sometimes even brutal honesty, is the only hope for struggling humanity. This search people are into leaves deep scars and hurt. Some of the hurt will never heal. Honesty with self, no matter how it hurts, is really the answer. There are six things that we must avoid in the struggle to be honest. Maybe someone you know has not been able to avoid some of these. These hurts are devastating, deep and lasting.

1. **Depraved thoughts, feelings or will.** When you are not honest with yourself the best you can hope for is "futility of thinking." Have you ever talked to someone who seemed to be losing his/her grip on proper thought processes? The person seemed to be slipping away from you, and you couldn't put your finger on why. It could be because of a lack of honesty with self.

"Thinking" here is from the Greek "(nous)" which means "thoughts, feelings, and will." When we are not honest with self it begins to work on, and eventually degenerate the entire "spirit" of one's personality.

The way to self-examine is simply to **notice the counsel of others.** If everyone in your family is telling you to avoid something, or warning you about something, it is possible that you are going in the wrong direction and don't even realize it. Listen to counsel. You may be down the road of futility and not know it. Be open with other's opinions and be honest with yourself.

2. Problems with your subconscious. "...darkened understanding..." "Understanding" here is (dianoia), meaning deep, deep thought. A lack of honesty with self is a condition of mental hiding. "Hiding" recesses into the subconscious mind. When these hidden feelings are not dealt with by being honest they are buried deeper into the subconscious. To help in the subconscious area, the answer is simple--be honest with yourself--but the application is extremely difficult. When something is in the subconscious, it is there because those feelings have never been dealt with. Honesty is not the best policy--it is the only policy!

3. A block in a spiritual life. "Separated from the life of God." There is so much more to being saved than just being saved! The spiritual journey requires constant care and consistent honesty with self. God wants our spiritual life to be a two-way relationship with him, but if we are not honest with ourselves, there cannot be a relationship. Honesty with self is one of the basic elements of spirituality. Without it there can never be things of the spirit like conviction, direction, sanctification and edification. There is a possibility that once in a while a person might be able to feel a hint of these works of the spirit, but these works of God will never develop in a person's life due to a lack of honesty with self.

It will take a step of faith from those who know that lack of honesty is their problem. But once they take that step, their spiritual life will never again be the same!

4. Thoughts and feelings become hardened. This point differs from the earlier point of thoughts and feelings degenerating morally and ethically—this is the hardening of thoughts and feelings.

Do you feel like you are hardening? Then there is something you are not being honest about with yourself. The Christian life should have just the opposite effect on us. We should be in a constant state of softening in our thoughts and feelings. Discovering the problem area will not be difficult. Honesty is initially produced in this area of thoughts and feelings. So if one is hardening, a softening could quickly be affected if honesty is applied.

5. Losing Sensitivity. Sensitivity is not emotional, it is mental. Being sensitive to others and being emotional are two different things. Sensitivity is really having an understanding for others. If we don't have sensitivity, we are handicapped in all human endeavors. The businessman needs sensitivity to marketing and people's needs. The salesman needs a sensitivity to close the sale. The housewife needs sensitivity to proper scheduling. By being sensitive, we can see prosperity and happiness. The only way to increase sensitivity is by being honest with self. When you are honest with yourself, you are developing sensitivity to self. This in turn helps in developing sensitivity for others.

6. The continual lust for more. We can really lust after anything. Anything! The point for which we need to be careful is "continual." We could continually be craving something, but if we have been dishonest with self, we might be covering up the continual lust as something else. How tragic it is to see people do exactly this until they reach moral failure, when they could have received help all along. We must be honest with self. You are the only one you can help in this area.

The basic place where honesty belongs is with honesty with self. These six pit falls must be avoided. The answer to each one of these problems and their resulting ramifications is simply to be honest with self.

Honesty with Self - The Application

"You, however, did not come to know Christ that way. Surely you heard of him in accordance with the truth that is in Jesus. You were taught, with regard to your former way of life, to put off your old self, which is being corrupted by its deceitful desires; to be made new in the attitude of your minds; and to put on the new self created to be like God in true righteousness and holiness." Ephesians 4:20-24

If you have never been honest with yourself—how can you do it? The text sets up a simple scenario for us, which is both practical and applicable. It is a simple three step process. However, I hope it is not too simple that we miss its impact.

Step #1—Put off old self. If you can see "self" as clothing, you can more adequately grasp this first concept. If you see the old self as a shirt which you have soiled, you can see yourself as tossing it into the laundry basket.

Use this simple visualization. The reason you can't be honest with yourself is because you have a problem with how you see yourself. Since this is the case--take off your self. Visualize it and you can achieve it!

Step #2—Let yourself be renewed. Since your clothes are off and you are naked, renew what you think of yourself. Renew (ananeoo) means to "renovate." The text infers the renewal must happen in the spirit of the mind. Mind (hous) means "meaning." We need to be renovated in our "meanings" or in how we perceive of events and circumstances. Don't be afraid of this essential second step. It is both relevant and necessary.

Step #3—Put on a new self. Put on (enduo) means sinking into a garment. Wear your renovated self like a plush, soft, new garment. Enjoy wearing it. If you have renovated yourself, you have been honest and actually have seen what honesty can do!

These three steps should be taken as often as necessary. It is not a one time only exercise. Anytime you are not being honest with yourself, walk through these three steps--even if it has to be done every hour for awhile!

HONESTY IN LIFE

When it comes right down to it, honesty is all we've got as people. It is the good will which honesty produces that gives us the essentials of a society. The economy exists only because of good will and honesty. Relationships with people exist only because of good will and honesty. Chapter four, verses 25-32 of Ephesians gives us several principles of honesty in life.

"Therefore each of you must put off falsehood and speak truthfully to his neighbors for we are all members of one body. In your anger do not sin; do not let the sun go down while you are still angry, and do not give the devil a foothold. He who has been stealing must steal no longer, but must work, doing something useful with his own hands, that he may have something to share with those in need."

"Do not let any unwholesome talk come out of your mouths, but only what is helpful for building others up according to their needs, that it may benefit those who listen. And do not grieve the Holy Spirit of God, with whom you were sealed for the day of redemption. Get rid of all bitterness, rage and anger, brawling and slander, along with every form of malice. Be kind and compassionate to one another, forgiving each other, just as in Christ God forgave you." Ephesians 4:25-32

This portion of the text gives us twelve outstanding principles for honesty. Each of them has a different emphasis and directive, but when faced with each, we must apply it as a principle for a life of honesty.

1. Avoid all forms of falsehood.

When we speak of lying, we have developed an intricate scenario for the degrees of falsehood. We call some "white lies", to distinguish them from lying. But to live a life of honesty, we must avoid all forms of falsehood. There are many, many different possibilities in this realm, but all these possibilities must be avoided at all costs.

Any attempt to mislead others should also be considered the bottom line when considering falsehood. There are dozens of ways to be false--to live a life of honesty we must avoid them all!

2. Speak accurately.

"Speak truthfully" gives us an imperative. This imperative breaks into every area of life, including relationships, circumstances and situations. "Truthful" becomes "accurately" when it relates to all the dynamics of the human endeavor. It can cause us to apply truthfulness more deeply than what has been traditionally thought.

Speaking accurately works two ways, by the way we communicate, and the way we understand. In our communication, we need to be clear and not beat around the bush, mislead, manipulate, or misrepresent.

Not only are we to speak accurately, we are to listen accurately. Develop yourself into an active listener. Clarify what is said. We must not misread, but listen closely.

3. Control your stress.

"Don't sin in anger." The concept of anger (orsro) means to provoke into exasperation. This clearly shows us that emotion in and of itself is not sin. The sin is in the lack of control of it. When one goes out of control, sin evolves. We have to place our stress under control. There are several things to do:

- **Realize your emotional limits.**

- **Know yourself.**

- **Develop ways to control unpredictable emotions brought on by stress.**

4. Don't give the devil an inch.

It just would not be appropriate to talk about a life of honesty without mentioning the evil one. It is the devil's goal to create dishonesty. The scenario he uses is slow and deliberate. If he can cause us to develop areas of dishonesty, starting small at first, then he is able to gain an area. Soon it builds and expands. "Don't give the devil a foothold" (topos) means a sport, or space, or condition.

The only way to avoid giving the devil a foot hold is by living a life of total honesty:

<u>Physically</u>, when you mess up, face up to it and repent.

<u>Mentally</u>, be honest with self, always.

<u>Spiritually</u>, allow the Holy Spirit to work.

5. Do things of value.

When your life has value, you will know it. When your life has value, you will do things of value. The scriptural concept here is "labor" (kapiao) which gives us the notion of good, hard, satisfying work--which also leaves one fatigued. This is often the kind of work called "honest work." Every Christian believer must resolve to do and say things of value. It is in this way we are able to live a life of honesty.

6. Say things of value.

"No unwholesome talk." Not only are we to do things of value, but we are also to say things of value. "Unwholesome" (phthio) means to "pine or waste away." If we are not saying things of value then our talk is degenerating. When we begin to say these valueless things, we soon develop a tendency for dishonesty.

If the Christian believer commits himself to saying only things of value--this is the greatest way to protect the life of honesty.

7. Build up others.

The Apostle has used his concept of architecture (oikodome), building a foundation and then a building on top of it, often. Now we reflect upon building up others as a way of a life of honesty. Honesty builds people. It does not always make them feel good, but it builds people. If we say something just to make someone feel good, even if it is dishonest, it does not build people. Doing what it takes to build people requires an absolute life of honesty!

8. Don't grieve the Holy Spirit.

This is strictly an opinion, but the greatest way we grieve the Holy Spirit is through our masks we wear. Many, many Christians are not real people, but are fakes. This kind of image portrayed is dishonest. Not only that, but it distresses the work of the Holy Spirit. Grieve (lupeo) means exactly that, to distress. Not being real people is dishonest and distresses the work of God through his Holy Spirit.

9. Don't take everything so seriously.

When we take our lives and ourselves too seriously we can become intense. The eventual outcome is too much passion. When we allow ourselves to take ourselves too seriously, we do things which are not always in line with the life of honesty. The scripture says we should "put it away," cast it off.

Kindness is an element of honesty. Brutal honesty is not really honest unless honesty is mixed with kindness. Kindness provides a necessary balance to a life of honesty. Honesty is never meant to be something to hurt people.

11. Compassion.

Compassion is very necessary especially for someone who wants to live a life of honesty. Compassion must be the guide for expressions of honesty.

12. Be forgiving.

The bottom line for the life of honesty is forgiveness. A forgiving spirit is also a necessary element of honesty. Forgiveness has to be evident to balance a life of honesty.

Chapter 8

REVERENCE

Reverence. It is that concept which has been the traditional title of the clergy. "Reverend," abbreviated Rev. is placed in front of the name of every minister who is ordained. But just what is this word, and why is it just applied to the ranks of the clergy?

Reverence is our eighth dirty word in the study of the book of Ephesians. Unfortunately reverence has been classified and categorized for just a group of people. Most of us don't see reverence as applicable for us today—it is just a dirty word!

But reverence is for us! Reverence is more powerful than mere concepts of respect, appreciation or even admiration. Reverence involves a substantial portion of all three.

Reverence is 80% appreciation for all of creation, 80% respect for all of creation, 80% admiration for how every thing works together. What does 240% mean? This is the power of reverence in life! It makes up more than just the whole—but 2½ of them!

The text in Ephesians 5:1-2 gives us four very interesting areas for reverence. Reverence for life found in verses 1 and 2, reverence for life principles in 5:3-7, reverence for life direction in 5:8-14, and reverence for lifestyle from 15-20. I cannot stress enough the importance of reverence in life. It is not hype, not a motivational pitch; it is truly a spiritual experience.

Reverence for Life

"Be imitators of God, therefore, as dearly loved children and live a life of love, just as Christ loved us and gave himself up for us as a fragrant offering and sacrifice to God." Ephesians 5:1-2

We must revere life. The description of this task may seem like "pie in the sky" at first, but as we examine the text, we see it is very practical. We show reverence for life in three ways, reverence for God, reverence for people and reverence for sacrifice.

Reverence for God: "Be imitators of God"

We can never show reverence for life until we show reverence for God. God is the basic key in the realm of reverence. Reverence for God must be the first thing we think about in the morning and the last thing we think about at night.

The text does not just raise the issue of reverence but it gives the directive of "how to" as well. It says be "imitators of God." Nothing could be simpler--do what God does! How do we know God? We know Him by knowing the Son. By studying Jesus we can see and develop the autobiography of God. Not only does this include a study of Christ, but it also includes application. Not only should we know God, we should be imitators of God. With continual studying, application and prayer, this can happen! It will happen!

Reverence for People: "Live a life of love."

This scriptural point deals with our relationship with others. With the same intensity as we demonstrate reverence for the Creator, we must have reverence for His creation. Every living thing is his creation and we must treat them as we would the creator. The dynamic of reverence for people is displayed in three ways:

1. We must show to every person the same respect, admiration, and appreciation (reverence) as we do to God. Many Christian believers make a sad mistake at this point: they seem to give God a high place and people no place. This arrogant spirit is wrong and has no place in the Kingdom of God.

2. We must show every living thing the same respect, admiration and appreciation (reverence) as we do to God. No kicking the dog or killing the cat! They are God's creation.

3. We must show the whole creative realm the same respect, admiration, and appreciation (reverence) as we do to God. This applies to our atmosphere and environment. We need to see conversation as a serious spiritual principle. The preservation of our world need not be left in the hands of the environmentalists, but the Christian believer must do his part as well!

This concept of reverence for people must be more than a challenge; it has to be an imperative.

REVERENCE FOR SACRIFICE

"Just as Christ loved us and gave himself up for us as a fragrant offering and sacrifice to God." 5:2

In World War II they had what was referred to as the Kamikaze pilots. These fighting machines were men who gave no thought of their own lives. They would fly their aircraft into cities and ships. They were killed with the rest, but their own life meant nothing in comparison to what their mission was. They were greatly feared and dangerous men.

Today, it is an entirely different story. We hold so tightly to our lives that we don't seem to band together enough to accomplish the spiritual impact God intends. We have denominations, doctrinal differences, Christian celebrities, $20 Christian books, millionaire preachers and carnal Christians.

But what was Jesus? He was a Christian Kamikaze. He gave his one life to redeem everyone's life. Would you die for Him? The only economy God has is the economy of sacrifice. Would you die for Him? Jesus said, whoever saves his life shall lose it, but whoever loses his life for my sake shall find it. Would you die for Him? If you would die for Him---Jesus asks you the question, would you live for me?

REVERENCE FOR LIFE PRINCIPLES

Not only are we to show reverence for life, but also for several life principles. I don't know if the context in Ephesians 4:3-7 is all encompassing in its "life principles, but I do know that if we work on these five principles, we won't have the time or the energy to worry about any more! These are some very challenging life principles, but they require diligent effort to show proper appreciation, respect and admiration (reverence) for them.

"But among you there must not even be a hint of sexual immorality, or any kind of impurity, or of greed, because these are improper for God's holy people. Nor should there be obscenity, foolish talk or coarse joking which is out of place, but rather thanksgiving. For of this you can be sure: No immoral, impure, or greedy person--such a man is an idolater--has any inheritance in the kingdom of Christ and of God. Let no one deceive you with empty words, for because of such things God's wrath comes on those who are disobedient. Therefore do not be partners with them." Ephesians 4:3-7

Principle #1: Show no hint of sexual immorality.

This first principle comes from the word fornication (porneia). This concept is built on a continuum. It begins from the right with the very hint of the pornographic, to all the way over to the left side of the spectrum which is the gross, most perverted forms of prostitution. We have sexual drive. It is part of the human physical and emotional make-up. It is important, but it can also be taken out of context in our lives and cause great damage. For instance, 95% of child molesters were molested as children. Everything in the realm of the sensual only grows and builds momentum. There is no stopping it until we finally draw a line and say that enough is enough. That is our reason for this principle in our reverence for life. We must actually have a deep reverence for the principle of life, which says we must not even have a hint of sexual impurity.

Principle #2: Don't have any form of uncleanness.

Is cleanliness next to godliness? According to our text it is! The concept of cleanliness (akatharsia) means both physical and moral cleanness. We must have a deep reverence for this principle of moral cleanness. This principle is not unlike our first principle as far as the momentum and propensity to create a larger and greater problem. Uncleanness creates laziness. Because of laziness, uncleanness becomes increasingly prevalent in a life of uncleanliness. We must nip the problem in the bud before it starts. Show a deep reverence for this life principle of valuing physical and moral cleaness.

Principle #3: Don't be greedy in any way.

Greed can be seen in a large variety of forms. Often greed is visible, yet many forms are secret. Principle number three includes all forms of greed. There are contemporary forms of greed like manipulation, as well as the traditional forms of greed like coveting things you wish to possess. We must show a deep reverence by avoiding greed of any kind.

Principle #4: Express and show gratitude easily.

Gratitude or a "thankful spirit" is an essential principle of life. This small principle could make one a success in life. Gratitude contains untapped potential. Gratitude is a magic that can only be revealed and felt as it is expressed.

The problem of ingratitude occurs when we acquire a higher opinion of ourselves than we should. When this occurs we begin to make untruthful assumptions about how deserving we are—because we truly do not deserve. We must view everything in life we enjoy as how undeserving we are...then we will begin to enjoy the supreme benefits of gratitude.

We must demonstrate a deep reverence for expressing and showing gratitude easily.

Principle #5: Be choosy about with whom you associate.

"Let no one deceive you with empty words!" Our friends are the ones who deceive us. We are so concerned about our young people and peer pressure when we could be being mislead right now by our own friends! They "delude by empty words," but we have little or no knowledge as to who this could be.

There is one test we can give to our friends. It comes from the concept of disobedient (apeitheia) which means "obstinate and rebellious." Do you have associates or friends who exhibit these faults? If you do, these people are the ones to avoid. We must have a deep reverence for being choosy about with whom our associates are and with whom we associate!

Here is the difficult part of this principle: The text infers that people who do not show reverence for these five principles have no inheritance in the Kingdom of Christ. This is a sobering fact. We must do well in all five of these principles!

REVERENCE FOR LIFE DIRECTION

If there could be three life directives God could speak to each of us personally, they are found in Ephesians 5, verses 8 through 14. These life directives are extremely serious business.

"For you were once darkness, but now you are light in the Lord. <u>Live as children of light</u> (for the fruit of the light consists in all goodness, righteousness and truth,) and <u>find out what pleases the Lord</u>. Have nothing to do with the fruitless deeds of darkness, but <u>rather expose them</u>. For it is shameful even to mention what is done in secret. But everything exposed by the light becomes visible, for it is light that makes everything visible. This is why it is said: Wake up, O sleeper, rise from the dead, and Christ will shine on you." Ephesians 5: 8-14

There are three absolute life directives: (1) Live as children of the light, (2) Find out what pleases the Lord, (3) Expose the deeds of darkness.

1. Live as children of the light.

This first directive requires our diligent concentration. That is why reverence (respect, appreciation and admiration) is essential. Living as children of the light is a Biblical directive.

There are two important aspects of this life directive—children and light. Children (teknon) mean a son or daughter.

Light (phos) means to illuminate. We are to live as if we are illuminated on our path of life. It shouldn't be hard to live in the way God provides! We must be honest and responsible to the illumination God has given each of us. Our responsibility is for self alone (individually). The illumination on others is of no concern to us—God works with the individual.

Finally, we are to live as children of the light. We are to live the illumination. We are to apply our illumination. It is our Biblical directive.

2. Find out what pleases the Lord.

The first life directive has to be in place before this second directive can be applied. The Christian believer must have a propensity to live in the light before one undertakes the journey which takes one on finding out what pleases the Lord.

This journey is one of testing the waters of safety. Many activities of our modern society are not specifically named in the Scripture. It is therefore imperative that Christian believers commit themselves to finding out what pleases the Lord by applying the following test. If the answers are "yes" then that activity should please the Lord--if "no" then it would not please the Lord.

- **Is this activity in line with the Spirit of Scripture?**

- **Can it be done with a clear conscious?**

- **Is it beneficial to the cause of Christ in some/any way?**

3. Expose the deeds of darkness.

This life directive is not just satisfied with avoiding the deeds of darkness, but it is also imperative to expose them as well. This concept is developed from the Greek word *elescho,* it means to "bring to a conviction." As militaristic as it sounds, it appears that we are to work at bringing works of darkness to a conviction.

Every Christian believer should really be creatively working on bringing works of darkness into a conviction. Although the ways are varied, the mission is clear; we must expose the deeds of darkness so that others will not be sucked into darkness.

We must show reverence for this life directive. It must be an imperative of our course of life. Exposing the deeds of darkness is not optional.

Live as children of light. Find out what pleases the Lord. Expose the deeds of darkness. All three are imperative, but difficult. It is with the utmost reverence that we must deal with these!

REVERENCE FOR LIFESTYLE

"Be very careful, then, how you live--not as unwise, but as wise, making the most of every opportunity because the days are evil. Therefore do not be foolish, but understand what the Lord's will is. Do not be drunk on wine, which leads to debauchery. Instead, be filled with the Spirit. Speak to one another with psalms, hymns, and spiritual songs. Sing and make music in your heart to the Lord, always giving thanks to God the Father for everything, in the name of our Lord Jesus Christ." Ephesians 5:15-20

The fourth and final area for reverence is that of lifestyle. With the emergence of a plethora of known lifestyle problems among Christian believers something needs to be applied to provide us with a deeper motivation to Christian lifestyle. Christian lifestyle is necessary for the concept of reverence. If we can be reverent about the seven areas mentioned in our text, we can achieve great victory in the areas of lifestyle.

1. Be careful how you live.

This first concept of Christian lifestyle provides a dimension to reverence. Being careful how you live is from the Greek word *akribos* which means to be exact. Exactness in life reveals itself in three ways: actions, attitudes and communication.

Christians must be exact in their actions. We must be careful what we do and where we go.

Christians must be exact in what they say. Our words are all we have to communicate to our world. We must be exact in our communication.

We must be exact in our attitudes. What we think we can become. Christian lifestyle begins, grows and is achieved in our thought processes.

2. Make the most of every opportunity.

"Redeeming the times" has been a traditional challenge from the King James Version. We must continually improve. We must work every opportunity! We must rescue from every loss!

Making the most of every opportunity is definitely a life-long prospect—it is a commitment which requires diligent application. The importance of making the most of every opportunity is especially evident in the fact that we need to show reverence for valuing time and using it wisely.

3. Understand what the Lord's will is.

To comprehend God's determination is the constant work of the Christian lifestyle. The point of trying to understand God's will is not to enable us to predict God, but to help the Christian believer to grow in personal acceptance of God's will in life.

Comprehending God's determination is a powerful notion, enough to be taken reverently.

4. Don't get drunk.

It is interesting to realize that intoxication is an age old problem. Alcohol is used as a crutch for people to cope with difficulties of their society, but God wants to be that crutch. God wants us to be dependent upon Him, not upon intoxicating beverages. The Greek word used here, *methush,* was not the legal blood alcohol limit by a highway patrol standard, but scripturally intoxication is any amount of intoxicating liquor that does <u>anything to the bloodstream</u>. Further, this concept in scripture illustrates that drunkenness leads to excess (asotia), which means "unreserved" or "unsavedly." Liquor causes this unreserved or unsaved behavior. However, God provides the alternative!

5. Be filled with the Spirit.

Point 5 works in tandem with point 4. "Instead, be filled with the Holy Spirit." "Filled" is from the Greek text (pleroo) meaning "cram your nets full." We need to be filled constantly and continually with the presence of God by his Holy Spirit. The only way this is ever done is by the diligent and reverent effort of every Christian believer.

The only way to live a life above your problems, situations and frustrations is by being filled with the Holy Spirit. It takes a moment by moment submission to the power of God in your life. As intense as it sounds, living with a moment by moment submission to God truly is the way for the lifestyle of the Christian believer.

6. Speak only positive things to one another.

Speak to one another with "psalms, hymns, and spiritual songs." It is obvious the only expression God desires between people is expressions of joy. It doesn't matter what these expressions and communications are as long as they are positive in content.

Further, we are to be positive within our own hearts as well! God does not want us to be centered in on any form of negativity. Only positive things are to be allowed in our thinking.

We are presented again with a very intense lifestyle concept which will require deep concentration and a deep spirit of reverence. This one point could change your life!

7. Express your gratitude.

This lifestyle principle is repeated from the earlier life principle. The apostle apparently wanted us to get this point! We must have a gracious spirit about everything and toward everyone. Then, we are to express that gracious spirit as well!

Closing out the eighth dirty word of reverence, the last few versus give us a rare glimpse into what God would like for us. He wants deeply for us to celebrate life through thanksgiving. How important it must be to God that we need not get bogged down in the pressures and stress of living. We were created to live in a garden. This garden existence would be one of celebration. The Greek word *hudos* (hymn) means to "celebrate." How different our lives would be if we could develop a melody in our hearts rather than a worrisome spirit. Reverence comes through a celebration of thanksgiving. Celebrate today!

Respect Issues:

1. We must show every human relationship the same respect, admiration, and appreciation (reverence) as we do to God.

2. We must show every living thing the same respect, admiration and appreciation (reverence) as we do to God.

3. We must show the whole creative realm the same respect, admiration, and appreciation (reverence) as we do to God.

Chapter 9

SUBMISSION

Dr. X was the developer and procurer of the figure-four leg lock. In the 1960's Dr. X was the masked bad guy of professional wrestling. He would wear down his opponent until he could put his peculiar leg lock on them to the point they would submit. They would yell in their pain, "I submit!" The referee would then call the match. It was extended to a broad challenge Dr. X made to people everywhere. If anyone could break his figure-four leg lock, he would pay them $5,000 and remove his mask to reveal his true identity. No one could break his hold— everyone had to submit by the intensity of the pain. Submission was the only way out of the pain for each. Some waited longer than others, but all had trouble enduring the pain.

Submission is the ninth dirty word in Ephesians. In chapter five we see the practice of submission in verse 21, the place of submission in verses 22-24, and the mystery of submission in verses 25-33. Through these three studies, the depth of submission is disclosed. Submission is a powerful concept which must demand the careful attention and application of every Christian believer.

"Wives, submit to your husbands as to the Lord—for the husband is the head of the wife as Christ is the head of the Church, his body, of which he is the Savior. Now as the church submits to Christ, so also wives should submit to their husbands in everything. Husbands love your wives just as Christ loved the Church and gave himself up for her to make her holy, cleansing her by the washing with water through the word, and to present her to himself as a radiant church, without stain or wrinkle or any other blemish, but holy and blameless. In this same way, husbands ought to love their wives as their own bodies. He who loves his wife loves himself. After all, no one ever hated his own body, but he feeds and cares for it, just as Christ does the church--for we are members of his body. For this reason a man will leave his father and mother and be united to his wife, and the two will become one flesh. This is a profound mystery--but I am talking about Christ and the Church. However each one of you also must love his wife as he loves himself and the wife must respect her husband." Ephesians 5:22-33

SUBMISSION: THE PRACTICE

"Submit to one another out of reverence for Christ." Ephesians 5:21

Submission is from the Greek word *hupotasso* which means to subordinate—to voluntarily bring oneself into subjection. Submission is completely and absolutely voluntary. If submission is not voluntary, then it is not submission. If it is forced, it is not submission. If it is demanded by a spouse or an employer, it is not submission. It might be **slavery**, but not **submission**. Whenever debate about submission begins, it has already ended. It is important that we come to terms with the realities to allow submission to do the work it needs to do in a life. Submission has to evolve in the heart of the Christian believer, completely voluntary, completely uncoached, completely from the Holy Spirit. Submission could cause a great stir in the heart of the Christian believer if the believer would see it as a spiritual need. On the other hand, submission can devastate human relationship by the carnal exercise of demanding submission. From the text, there are three important concepts for us to see concerning the practice of submission.

1. Submission is necessary for the organization of groups.

If no one submitted to leadership, there would be no organization. To achieve spiritual success a church, (the Church) must practice submission. Members of the body of Christ must subordinate themselves voluntarily to create the living, growing, vibrant body that Christ intends. As Christian believers we are parts of the body of Christ. We are parts of Christ by name only unless we voluntarily submit ourselves to the head.

Submission is the key to the Church. Many, many churches are churches in name only. The reason they are not true churches is because the members have not submitted to the head. In this condition and state the church is simply a sociological unit, far less than the life changing body Christ intended—but definitely the look of it. When it looks like the Church—but doesn't feel like the Church—it is not the Church. The reason: submission is missing!

2. Submission is a means to an end, not an end in itself.

Submission is a tool in the hands of God. It is a tester of our spiritual commitment. We are often too intense regarding submission and hence miss the value of it. Submission is the prompter of a spiritual experience, because submission is a spiritual experience. It is the exact opposite of rebellion. Rebellion was the problem of original sin. Eve rebelled against God's command. We see no signs that Eve ever did submit. Submission is God's gift to us by providing a directive to avoid rebellion.

3.   Submission can only be applied and preserved among Christian believers.

"Out of ...fear of God." Submission to one another is tied to God.   To properly execute it, we must apply submission to Christian believers.   The proper Biblical model works only when Christians are involved.   We have often become discouraged when we submit to a non-Christian employer or spouse and don't see the result submission was intended to have.   It can only be properly observed in the ranks of Christian believers.   It is in this environment that submission truly becomes a spiritual work.

Submission must be practiced.   It takes careful and sincere searching and then proper execution to see the marvelous transformation submission can bring to the body of Christ.

THE PLACE/REASON OF/FOR SUBMISSION

Using the text presented, the most natural response to the title of this section, "the place of submission" would be the home.   The home, however, is much too limiting to see Ephesians 5:22-24 as an admonition to wives only. We must broaden our view of submission to see the frequent inference that the marital union is symbolic as Christ and the Church.   The tendency through the years has been to place the emphasis on submission, even heavy emphasis, upon the wife-husband relationship; whereas a deeper look shows us that the marital relationship becomes only a parallel and example of the deeper concept of the place of submission. If we objectively examine the text in its context we see the place of submission in three guidelines—in "as to the Lord"; in "headship"; in "everything." We can quickly turn these three notions from the place of submission into the reasons for submission. In light of the text, the places for submission and the reason for submission are one and the same.

Submission Must be Seen with Perspective

In some households this relational aspect will never be able to occur. In many cases if a wife would submit herself to her husband--he would have no concept of the Biblical notion of submission. It would seem like slavery, and most non-Christian husbands would love that arrangement!

"As unto the Lord" is the whole key to this principle of submission. This gives the Christian believer a heavenly mandate to submit voluntarily. If this does not happen there can be no pressure exerted because if there is--it would nullify the whole purpose of the work of submission.

It is at this point we separate the two concepts:

Wives submit to husbands. The Apostle is very precise—in his writings—in his observation of the needs of men and women (aner and gune in the Greek text). He tries to provide women with a sense of security, self-worth, and protection. The focus is very admirable and accurate. The thing a wife must do to achieve a sense of security, self worth, and protection is to voluntarily give herself to her husband and allow him to care for her. This is in no sense slavery or the life of the servant girl. Additionally, every Christian believer must submit in the same way to God, which transitions to the second division.

The Church submits to Christ. Every Christian believer is the Church. Every Christian believer must come to the place of voluntarily giving themselves to Christ to care, protect, and provide. Submission can be a celebration of life.

Submission Must Be Lived Out Constantly

Headship is the second place of and reason for submission. We see an organizational hierarchy in the Apostle's short chain of command—"the husband is the head of the wife as Christ is head of the Church." Head, (kapto), is defined as the sense of seizing, the one who is easily taken a hold of. Headship does not project anything glamorous about it at all. In the old television war program of the 1950's, "Combat," headship could be easily illustrated from the men with higher ranks. When time came for promotions all the men turned them down or did something disrespectful to avoid a higher rank, as they did not want to assume the extra responsibility.

Headship has a price to be paid. Jesus Christ paid the price. He is, and always will be the head. Headship means Christ is responsible for the Christian believer. It also means the husband is responsible for the welfare of his wife---because why? Christ is responsible for him. With proper application we could turn this misinterpretation of headship around forever!

Submission Must Be Applied To Everything

In the last portion of Ephesians 5, verse 24, we see that the church must submit to Christ and wives to their husbands---in everything.

Everything is a unique concept. The Greek text divides this into two words--every (pas) meaning anything and everything, and "thing" (nupsoma) means an elevated place or thing.

It is with the concept of hupsoma (thing) that we see the ultimate reason for this Biblical imperative of submission. To voluntarily bring oneself into subjection is for the purpose to bring down any elevated place, object, or relationship in one's life.   God does not allow the Christian believer to elevate anything other than Jesus. Idolatry is the act of elevation.   We must not allow anything to come between us as believers and God. Submission is God's gift to keep that from happening!

THE MYSTERY OF SUBMISSION

The marital relationship is symbolic of that mystical relationship between Christ and his church.   The entire text is relative to submission, and for us submission is as much a mystery as Christ and his church.   Mystery (mysterion) means to "shut the mouth." This shows us that the facts are known about the mystery but not revealed to us.   The reasons for a mystery are varied, but always in God's case, a mystery is a mystery for our own good.

Husbands' loving their wives is the parallel in the text of Ephesians 5, verses 25-33.   This part of the marital relationship is even more intense than the previous

105

section. Love (agapao) is an intense love in both the social and moral sense. This love concept is the ultimate form of what submission is--the relationship of husband/wife which places emphasis on the dynamic of the husband's commitment:

Give himself up. Christ, indeed, gave himself totally to the Church. He did it for several reasons:

1. To make her holy. Holiness never comes without sacrifice.

2. To cleanse her. There could never have been any purging and purifying except by Christ.

3. To present to himself a radiant church. It is especially interesting to note that all this was done to give back to himself. The same is true of a husband to his wife. If you want something changed in your relationship, change how you see it and it will be changed.

He who loves his wife loves himself. In the marital union two are made as one, the same is true of Christ and his church. We are one with Him.

Two will become one flesh. When we become Christian believers we turn all our cares over to Christ because he cares for every part of his body. When we marry, we turn our cares and concerns over to each other. This is the purpose of marriage.

It is important in marriage preparation to marry only the person whom you can become one with in all areas. Consistent and clear education must take place at a very early age for our young people to date and go steady with and solid Christian believers. We must vow our hearts only to those whom are worthy to take our trust.

The same becomes true of our relationship with the Savior. This relationship should only be entered into with care and submission. The trust we place in Christ will meet every need in our lives!

Chapter 10

OBEDIENCE

What do the childhood games "Mother, May I?" and "Simon Says" have in common? The theme of each game has to do with the tenth dirty word from the book of Ephesians, **obedience**. In "Mother May I?" permission must be obtained, and in "Simon Says" precise obedience is the key. Considering the importance obedience has in our lives, it is good that children play games that model its importance.

Yet obedience still is a dirty word in our society. It has lost its meaning and given way to rebellion. In Chapter six, verses 1 - 4 we see the importance of obedience in a scenario developed by the Apostle for children. The substance of the text is so helpful that it is being expanded to show the qualities of obedience in verses one through three, and the reason for obedience in verse four.

"Children obey your parents in the Lord, for this is right. Honor your Father and Mother—which is the first commandment with a promise that it may go well with you and that you may enjoy long life on the earth. Fathers do not exasperate your children; instead, bring them up in the training and instruction of the Lord." Ephesians 6:1-4

THE ELEMENTS OF OBEDIENCE

Everyone has had a parental relationship. Although this is no new deepening truth, it is an important concept to visualize. The Apostle is developing neutral ground to allow all of us to relate to "Children obey your parents." Obey (hupakono) means to "listen attentively and heed to a command." Children in the original text mean "the one produced." From the word study of children, we are able to see that this parent/child relationship described can be broadened to include both actual parent/child relationships, as well as implied parent/child relationships. Some of these implied parent/child relationships are Jesus/believer, pastor/parishioner, employer/employee (in some instances). Each of these implied relationships requires obedience. There are four elements of obedience which we can apply to both the actual parent/child relationship--and the implied parent-child relationship. These are ground out from the text:

1. Obedience requires attentive listening and proper execution. vs. 1 "Children obey your parents."

The original word obey: (hupakouo) gives us two clear admonitions concerning obedience. To be truly obedient, both of these components need to be executed. We cannot divorce the two.

Attentive Listening. To obey, we must listen first. This is not just being attentive—but actually listening for understanding. Attentive listening is never a natural practice. It requires spiritual commitment to listen attentively—but it also requires spiritual commitment to be obedient. Attentive listening is the natural beginning to spiritual obedience.

Proper Execution. If all we do is listening, we are never fully obedient. Once we understand, then we must execute what we have heard. This second part of the execution of instruction is what seals in obedience. In tandem with obedience then, is courage. Courage to execute brings the spiritual obedience necessary in the life of the Christian believer.

2. Obedience develops equitable character and balanced actions.

"For this is right"

The scripture says obedience is right—and right (diakaios) describes character. The conceptualization of obedience is with character. Character is what is missing in our society. Obedience is the answer to most of our problems.

There is powerful redeeming value in obedience. The redemption comes through the refinement created in a life of obedience. The ultimate fruit of obedience is in actions. Obedience refines to create a volume of valuable actions.

This second element of obedience needs to be a top priority for every Christian believer--equitability of character and balanced actions are a must!

3. Obedience is only possible by focusing.

"Honor your father and mother."

"Honor" (timao) is a focusing term. It means to prize or to fix a valuation on someone or something. To obey, we must prize the thing or the person we are obeying. This element of obedience is imperative. Focusing this single element is the most helpful in the "how to" part of obedience. If there is any problem with obedience then it becomes essential to focus in on the person or thing to which we are to be obedient. In this focus—create a great value on it. When this value is created, the motivation for obedience is increased substantially. Focusing may require some concentration, but it is imperative that we focus.

4. Obedience creates both a greater quality and quantity of life!

"Honor your mother and father—which is the first commandment with a promise—that it may go well with you and that you may enjoy long life on the earth." vs. 2, 3

Obedience creates one long-lasting feeling that nothing else can compare to—peace, satisfaction and fulfillment. How can this be explained? How can something with which we rebel so easily against be the very key to deep and abiding satisfaction? The answer: Obedience is a promise of God! Obedience is the only spiritual concept with an earthly promise. That promise is clear—both quality and quantity of life. Do you live an unfulfilled, unsatisfied, confused existence? If you are ready to change it, commit yourself to spiritual obedience. Are you ready?

PERSONAL REASONS FOR OBEDIENCE

"Fathers do not exasperate your children; instead, bring them up in the training and instruction of the Lord." Ephesians 6:4

Here is the warning to every parent. Don't frustrate your children through your ego, nagging, pride, carnality, embarrassment, humiliation, or teasing. If these occur the work of obedience will never occur in the life of the kids.

"Instead" there are three things we must do. These three things can also be seen as <u>personal reasons for obedience</u>.

1. **Bring them up.** "Ektrepho" means, "to rear up into maturity." Obedience brings maturity. The scenario of obedience creates the model for the maturation process because it causes one to stretch and grow. It is one of the very important reasons why obedience has to take place.

2. **Training.** "Paideia," the term, means disciplinary correction. Obedience also creates the atmosphere for correction. Disciplinary correction is necessary for anyone to discontinue in a cycle of wrongdoing. If we are never corrected, we will never know where to change, nor will we know how to change.

3. **Instruction.** This term (nonthesia) means, "calling attention to."

Obedience creates a "magnifying glass." Through obedience, details we might not have considered are brought to light. This is most important in our lives. Sometimes it hurts, but the magnifying glass is very necessary!

Maturation, disciplinary correction, and personal attention are all noble reasons for obedience. Any of these can change a person's life. When one is obedient—nothing remains the same.

Chapter 11

COMMITMENT

One of the outstanding speakers in America today is a motivational speaker known as Charles "Tremendous" Jones. In his opening he usually summons up humorous, yet startling anecdotes about the work place. Just as his listeners feel the penetrating conviction that something is missing in their work place, Charles "Tremendous" Jones tells them in a deep, guttural voice and proclaims with clenched fists:

"Com - mit - ment!!"

Commitment is Charles "Tremendous" Jones' answer to all their problems. And, as he speaks it becomes obvious that he has cut through much of the hype and motivational jargon that one usually hears. Commitment is the bottom line. Often it is one of the major things we avoid, which is why we call commitment the 11th dirty word in Ephesians.

Commitment is a powerful concept that is overlooked because people want easier answers. Some years ago I was counseling a couple who were having very complicated marital trouble. Both were divorced and remarried. Each had three children, as well as one together. "Yours, mine and ours," provided them with enough problems, but to top it off the two of them had virtually no relationship. They would call at all hours. I would usually drop what I was doing and see them. On one particular occasion I was very, very busy when they called, yet they insisted I had to see them. When I opened

113

the door, the wife had come by herself. As she shared the story was the same. They had an argument over something. It became heated, and words were exchanged which should not have been said. She was hurting very badly. I don't know if it was because I was tired of their problems, or that God moved upon me, but I said, "Okay now—for better or worse, for richer or poorer, in sickness and in health. Which is it?" She immediately became hysterical—no one ever mentioned commitment to her.

Commitment is our answer.

In times of war, soldiers "dig in." They dig foxholes and trenches. They are there to the end. "Digging in" during a battle is what commitment is in life.

In Chapter 6:5-9, we see our text for commitment. The primary purpose of the passage is commitment in the work place, yet it can be applied to the various places in our lives. In verses 5-8 we see "How commitment is possible anywhere." In verse 9, we see three concepts for masters.

HOW COMMITMENT IS POSSIBLE

"Slaves, obey your earthly masters with respect and fear, and with sincerity of heart, just as you would obey Christ. Obey them not only to win their favor when their eye is on you, but like slaves of Christ, doing the will of God from your heart. Serve wholeheartedly, as if you were serving the Lord, not man, because you know that the Lord will reward everyone for whatever good he does, whether he is slave or free." Ephesians 6:5-8

Commitment is possible! If you are the Christian believer that God wants you to be, you need to possess commitment. It must become a part of your life! The context gives us four principles whereby commitment is possible in our lives.

1. Commitment is only possible when you see that the one over you has been put there by Christ.

"Slaves obey your earthly masters with respect and fear and with sincerity of heart, just as you would obey Christ." vs. 5

A master (kurios) is one who is supreme in authority. This concept occurs in many, many arenas whenever someone surprises someone else. Hierarchy is how God created the world. No matter who you are, if you live in this world or the one to come, we will all have masters. It is God's intention for us never to be free and independent of all authorities, but to develop in our life the realm of commitment.

It is not enough just to verbalize commitment. There are four things we must work on to become committed in the way God expects.

Respect. We are to respect those in authority over us. If they are godless, then pray for them. If there are things in their lives which you just cannot respect, then find other areas in which you can respect them.

Fear. Fear has become an unpopular word. We try to change it, mask it, perfume it, but fear is fear. Certain amounts of fear are important!

<u>Sincerity</u>. Commitment comes in different levels and each level varies in its intensity. Sincerity has to be the basis of any level of any intensity.

Just as we would Christ. When we have a hard time with a leader, then our commitment to Christ must kick in and take over. It is God's will that this occur.

2. Commitment is possible when it is motivated by sincerity.

"Obey them not only to win their favor when their eye is on you, but like slaves of Christ, doing the will of God in your heart." vs. 6

The motivation of one's sincerity is key. When motivation of commitment is just to keep a good job or a good relationship that is advantageous personally, then the motivation is wrong, shallow and weak.

Commitment is not a show. It is a symbol of a deep spiritual life of sincerity. The only acceptable reason for commitment is a sincere heart motivated by a desire to do God's will. Commitment is God's will!

3. Commitment is only possible when it is done as "unto the Lord."

"Serve wholeheartedly as if you were serving the Lord, not men." vs. 7

Commitment is first and foremost a spiritual work! Each of our lives is different—each with a different destiny. Our lives of commitment must be seen as a vital part of the life of a Christian believer.

4. Commitment is only possible when you see that you are accountable.

"Because you know that the Lord will reward everyone for whatever good he does, whether he is slave or free." vs. 8

Through commitment there is an award system. Commitment keeps us accountable. The way many Christian believers act, they don't even realize they are accountable. It is not wrong that accountability is a motivator to commitment, as long as accountability is a means to an end rather than an end in itself. **The end in itself is commitment.**

THREE CONCEPTS FOR MASTERS

"And masters, treat your slaves in the same way. Do not threaten them, since you know that he who is both their master and yours is in heaven and there is no favoritism with him." vs. 9

In the same context--masters—those having authority, need to know a few things. In our society we often forget that those with more responsibility are more accountable for what they do and say as well. Clearly, "To him whom much is given, much is required." Masters in every area are solemnly accountable to God.

There are three imperatives for masters that apply in any setting which are borne out in the text.

1. Christ likeness and Christ-lightness.

"And masters treat your slaves in the same way."

All these previous concepts of commitment to the master, the master must apply to the slaves as well!

>(a) The master must see his/her responsibility as a spiritual commitment.

>(b) The master must perform his/her duties as "unto the Lord."

>(c) The master must be motivated only out of sincerity for God's will.

>(d) The master must be solemnly accountable to God.

2. Don't be a menace.

"Do not threaten them"

Threatening (apede) means to be a "menace." Sometimes power corrupts. This is what often happens with people in charge; they begin to operate in the flesh and not by the spirit. This becomes a menace to those under their charge. The scriptural charge strictly forbids a master to menace anyone under their charge.

3. Fairness.

"Since you know that he who is both their master and yours is in heaven, and there is no favoritism with him."

This part of the text should serve as a continual humbler for every master. There is someone always over another, with the Lord Jesus over everyone and everything.

118

Every master must be fair with all, especially with those under, not showing any favoritism.

Every "slave" and every "master" must exhibit commitment. This kind of commitment can truly only be ours by a spiritual experience, the kind that is totally God-centered.

"COMMITMENT" IS AS SCARY OF A WORD AS IT IS A "DIRTY WORD!"

****

Chapter 12

COURAGE

The final dirty word in our study of the book of Ephesians is one of great help and encouragement. Courage is the concept found in Ephesians 6:10-18.

Courage is a dirty word today because of the tendency of the natural man to succumb to peer-pressure, trends, fads, gossip, and public opinion. Courage is a spiritual work in the life of the Christian believer. It is the necessary element which will sustain the soul of the Christian believer in a day to day spiritual journey.

There are two definite categories of courage in the passage. The first category is courage to face the unknown, found in vs. 10-12. The second category is courage to face the needs of life as found in vs. 13-18. If you need courage, these are the passages to drink in. If courage is a dirty word to you or has been a dirty word, then these passages need to become part of your life!

COURAGE TO FACE THE UNKNOWN

"Finally, be strong in the Lord and in his mighty power. Put on the whole armor of God so that you can take your stand against the devil's schemes. For our struggle is not against flesh and blood, but against the rulers, against the authorities, against the powers of this dark world and against the spiritual forces in the heavenly realms."
Ephesians 6:10-12

The passage clearly shows us the power of evil. With this illustration, we are able to develop three powerful principles which give us the courage to face tomorrow, every tomorrow, as well as everything out there which is unknown.

1. Remove yourself from the picture—hide behind God.

"Be strong in the Lord and in his mighty power. Put on the full armor of God so that you can take your stand against the Devil's schemes.

Throughout scripture it is clear. We must lose our self to gain Christ. We must remove our self to gain eternal life. The text supports this thought. The only way to be powerful is through his power alone.

Even as a Christian believer we are not as strong as we think. To stand strong, we are absolutely admonished to put on God's armor. In ourselves we are defenseless. Defenselessness is a position that every Christian believer faces sometime in his/her life. Generally, it is not a bad position in which to be, for it finally dawns on us to stand in the power of God's might.

2. Realize the struggle is constant.

"For our struggle..."

Struggle originally came from two words, *eschatos* and *pale*. These words combined bring out the notion of a constant shaking up. As we reach for courage for the unknown, we must constantly realize that the shaking up has no real relief. Our spiritual being is strengthened through those ongoing struggles of life. In times of struggle, we are forced to remain close to God. By having this kind of dependency we are able to face the unknown.

3. Respect the power of evil.

"Not against flesh and blood, but against rulers, against the authorities, against the powers of this dark world and against the spiritual forces of evil in heavenly places." Ephesians 6:12-13

We should never cower to, or give in to the evil one, but we must have a healthy respect for the evil one. This respect for the power of evil must include four things:

(a) **The power of evil is chief in many arenas.** The word principalities (arche) demonstrate for us the concept of chief or one in charge. The respect for the power of evil <u>must</u> show discernment toward <u>power</u> structures. Many power structures are created for evil purposes.

(b) **The power of evil is forceful.** The force behind evil is invisible. A healthy respect for evil will help us safeguard times when we could be careless.

(c) **The power of evil is often hard to discern.** Darkness (skotos) means obscurity. The respect for the power of evil will help the Christian believer to make an important differentiation on who is the devil!

(c) **The power of evil is in high places.** A good respect for evil will show us that we need not be disillusioned when a fellow believer's faith falters because evil is in the highest of high places.

The future is imminent! To be the Christian believer each of us needs to be, we must face the future with courage...and we can!

THE COURAGE TO FACE THE NEEDS OF LIFE

"Therefore put on the full armor of God so that when the day of evil comes you may be able to stand your ground and after you have done everything to stand, stand firm then, with the belt of truth girded around your waist with the breastplate of righteousness in place, and with your feet fitted with the readiness that comes from the gospel of peace. In addition to all this take up the shield of faith with which you can extinguish all the flaming arrows of the evil one. Take the helmet of salvation and the sword of the Spirit, which is the word of God. And pray in the Spirit on all occasions with all kinds of prayers and requests. With this in mind, be alert and always keep on praying for all the saints." Ephesians 6:13-18

The armor described is very much an appropriate study for enrichment of the Christian life. This armor touches upon the needs of the human endeavor. We all have needs in our lives. We have both basic needs and personal needs. The general needs are needs that all of us have. But the personal needs are individual, personal. They differ from person to person, but are very real and valid. No matter what the need is, general or personal it can be met--but only if we have the courage to face those needs of life!

The armor of God is split into five areas of need. These needs have been around since the beginning of time. God created our needs so He could meet them. He will do exactly that--if we let him. Here are five needs, and the help we receive from God's armor to meet them.

1. Sexual needs.

"with the belt of truth around your waist."

"Waist" is the NIV term for that the KJV called "loins." The area of the body might be the same, but the Greek word (ophus) is quite intense. The notion of ophus is the parts with the procreative power. As graphic as it may seem, this is an inference to sexual drive.

Sexual drive has been often misconceived. To hear many talk, this sexual drive is an uncontrollable demon or a runaway steam locomotive. Most of the time, sexual drive is given too much credit and leeway. We do have a sexual drive, but God has given us a brain to stay in control, and the **courage** to keep it in control. To that end, we are responsible to keep it in control.

Where we are weak, He is indeed made strong. God has a special piece of armor to help us, a protector around our lower parts of truth. Truth (aletheno) means to speak or tell the truth. As we are honest with ourselves and truthful always with others, the sensual temptations in our lives can be cared for. It is when we are dishonest with ourselves and cover up our true feeling that we begin to succumb to sensual desires. Because of our desire, we justify our behavior. Every Christian believer must be committed to putting this belt of truth as the scripture says, "all around the waist." Completely and totally covered by truth will prevent sexual problems.

2. Psychological needs.

"With the breastplate of righteousness in place."

The breastplate was worn by the high priest and he would show off. He would stick out his chest like a rooster, strutting about to gain the attention of others. It was well known that the breastplate represented the pride or ego of the wearer. We all were given an ego by God as kind of a self-defense mechanism. Just as every animal has some form of defense, ours is a psychological one--the ego. The problem with the ego is that it becomes out of balance through depravation of psychological needs. God's armor to help us through this is the breastplate of righteousness. Righteousness (dikaisune) means equitability of character. Every psychological problem can be taken care of through the equitability of character. Righteousness is the plain and simple answer to psychological needs. Developing character is a difficult and tedious journey. It takes one down the roads of life. Character development occurs during every bump and grind along the way. Put on the breastplate of righteousness and meet your psychological needs.

3. Need to belong.

"And with your feet fitted with the gospel of peace as a firm footing."

Man can live 40 days without food, three days without water, three minutes without air, but only one second without hope. We have to belong. We have to feel needed. It is a deep and pressing need of the human endeavor.

125

It is with this need in mind that we see God providing us with armor. The concept of fitted (hupodeo) means to bind under one's feet. Peace (eirene) means prosperity because of peace. These are two very important concepts we must apply to meet this need in ourselves and in others:

First, we must be in unity with others. We must be able to be a team player. As Christians, we must be able to both follow and lead.

Second, we must be at peace with others. That takes backbone and backing down. It requires both patience and strength.

Applying these two concepts gives us the footing we need.

4. Spiritual needs.

"Take up the shield of faith with which you can extinguish all the flaming arrows of the evil one."

"Shield" here means an immensely large shield with a door shape. This protects thoroughly all parts of the body of the warrior and allows space to breathe as well. This was designed to protect completely.

Such is the importance of spiritual protection in the world today. We have many, many spiritual needs of which we have no idea. Only the Holy Spirit knows us entirely, including our spiritual needs.

The fiery darts of the devil zap us of strength and steal our joy. Without the shield in place we can die a slow and tortuous spiritual death. The original word for dart can mean a missile, dart or spear--all the treachery of warfare.

The only answer is the shield. This shield which meets our every spiritual need is plain and simply the Holy Spirit. By being filled with the Holy Spirit, even filled to overflowing, the shield protects us from all danger and harm. It is an imperative for the Christian believer to seek and receive!

5. Mental needs.

"Take the helmet of salvation and the sword of the Spirit, which is the word of God."

We are tempted, tossed, teased, and tested in many different ways. The place the devil gets to us first is mentally. All decisions of life are made mentally. Our minds are the center of what we do or don't do, of what we think about or don't think about.

Our mental needs are immense. It has an appropriate armor--the helmet. Helmet means to completely circle the head. Salvation (soterion) means defender or defense. Our responsibility is clear. We must protect our minds, through the sword of the Spirit, the word of God. Drinking in the Word of God is the ultimate in mental protection. The Word of God is our salvation, and our salvation is our helmet!

"With this in mind, be alert and always keep praying for all the saints..." Courage is a spiritual experience as well as a spiritual process. Courage and the armor of God are basic essentials for every Christian believer.

CONCLUSION

"Pray also for me, that whenever I open my mouth, words may be given me so that I will fearlessly make known the mystery of the gospel, for which I am an ambassador in chains. Pray that I may declare it fearlessly, as I should. Tychicus, the dear brother and faithful servant in the Lord, will tell you everything so that you also may know how I am and what I am doing. I am sending him to you for this very purpose that you may know how we are, and that he may encourage you. Peace to the brothers and love with faith from God the Father and the Lord Jesus Christ. Grace to all who love our Lord Jesus Christ with undying love."

"Dirty words" is a graphic term for a Biblical study. In the context of what we were trying to accomplish in the life of the Christian believer, we might not be strong enough in the title. These twelve "dirty words" are truly absolute imperatives in the life of every believer.

The Apostle concludes his letter with a request of prayer. This prayer is very appropriate. It has not only practical application, but personal application as well.

1. **Whenever I open my mouth, words may be given to me.** Having the tongue under control is the ultimate in scriptural yielding. Our tongue is usually the last thing to be submitted to God.

2. **That I may declare the Gospel fearlessly.** These early believers paid a high price for spreading the good news—even as high as their own lives. This is a powerful request by the Apostle. He knew, however, what he was asking—courage and fearlessness.

3. **Accept my faithful servant.** Tychicus was one of the Apostle's special groups of faithful servants. Paul could not be everywhere at once, so he utilized others. It is important that Christian believers listen to God's servants. God's plan has always been to use people.

****

Make these twelve dirty words work in your life!

(1) **Thankfulness—1:15-23**
(2) **Grace—2:1-10**
(3) **Unity—2:11-22**
(4) **Trust—3:1-13**
(5) **Growth—3:14-21**
(6) **Consistency—4:1-16**
(7) **Honesty—4:17-32**
(8) **Reverence—5:1-21**
(9) **Submission—5:22-33**
(10) Obedience—6:1-4
(11) Commitment—6:5-9
(12) Courage—6:10-20